AN HISTORICAL GUIDE TO QUÉBEC

by
Yves TESSIER

LA SOCIÉTÉ HISTORIQUE DE QUÉBEC

Fier passé oblige

SOCIÉTÉ HISTORIQUE DE QUÉBEC

Québec

Cover:

View from the Citadel of Québec
(Print by R. Wallis, sketch W.H. Bartlett,
Canadian Scenery Illustrated of N.P. Willis,
London 1832).

Picture courtesy:
Archives de la Ville de Québec,
collection iconographique A-H5200

Translated by: Frank Hogg

Legal deposit — Bibliothèque nationale
Third quarter 1991
ISBN 2-92-0069 41-1

Acknowledgements

We would like to express our gratitude to family and close friends who have encouraged us and have accepted our frequent absences during the preparation of this work. We would also like to extend our special thanks to Céline Boivin and Marc Beaudoin, who were the first to believe in this project; to the members of the reading committee of the Société historique de Québec, Abbé Honorius Provost, Camille Rousseau, and Roland Pelletier; and to G.H. Dagneau, Abbé Jean-Marie Thivierge, and Yvan Roy for their invaluable remarks and suggestions.

Pen-and-ink drawings were done by *Cécile Richard*.

*On the occasion of the
eightieth birthday
of Marie-Aimée Hamelin,
a great Québécoise.*

Preface

Who has not dreamed of discovering the soul of a city or country he or she is visiting. Unfortunately, with our insatiable curiosity, limited resources, and with so much to see, we often have to content ourselves with a rapid, superficial visit to the sites, spiced with a few gastronomical stops which, however, do not satisfy our hunger for information.

The Société historique de Québec and the author have taken up the challenge to offer you this tourist guide which will allow you to get to know the city of Champlain as it has been shaped by the people and their ideas and techniques over the three hundred and seventy-five years of its history. Yves Tessier, professor of history at Collège François-Xavier-Garneau, has succeeded in his task and invites you to discover the "hidden" Québec — what lies behind its charming facades and decor. Both visitor and resident, alike, will discover Québec as the gateway to a continent, as the capital of a colonial empire that stretched from the Atlantic to the Rockies and from Hudson's Bay to the Gulf of Mexico, and as the cradle of Catholicism in North America. Following the English conquest, Québec came under the influence of new cultures and religions. The city appears to us today as it has been shaped by les Québecois. Québec's charms are not always evident at first sight; the city should be savoured like a fine wine.

This guidebook thus serves as an original addition to the usual literature that is offered to us. It allows the visitor to come to grips with the many facets of our city. The Société historique de Québec is proud to present Mr. Tessier's *An Historical Guide to Québec*. We hope you will find it as valuable as we have in your quest to discover (or, perhaps, rediscover) Québec.

Marc Beaudoin
President
Société historique de Québec

Table of Contents

Introduction

Québec City has been blessed by nature. Since the beginning, the magnificence of the city has inspired admiration. Even Frontenac, the impetuous Governor of New France, was charmed by the site. He was supposed to have declared, "I have never seen anything as beautiful or as magnificent as Québec. There could be no better site for the capital of a future empire." At the beginning of this century, Wilfrid Laurier, Canada's Prime Minister, concluded that Québec City was unique. "Québec's charm," he said, "comes from the unexpected variety of its horizons; with each step, the scene changes, and a new panorama unfolds before your eyes, as delightful as the preceding one, yet nonetheless different...." Since that time, the city has won over increasing numbers of admirers. Each year, more than a million visitors stay, on the average, two to four days.... This book is dedicated to them.

Through a series of anecdotes written in an easy-to-understand manner, this souvenir guidebook aims at giving the reader on overall perspective of the history of Québec City without being an exhaustive study. The first chapter provides a brief summary of the important moments in the city's history. The second chapter, which constitutes the main part of this guidebook, includes a guided tour of Old Québec. This tour is divided into two parts of approximately equal length and duration. The complete itinerary is less than ten kilometres long and can be covered in a single day. The tourist, winding his or her way through the city's streets, is led to certain sights chosen for their historical interest or the panoramic view they offer of the city. A short text accompanied by an illustration describes the monument or the sight and explains the historical significance of each location. From one stop to the next, the visitor discovers the highlights of the city's history from the time of the Amerindians right up to the present. The Vieux-Port (Old Port) initiates the visitor to the maritime history of the city; the Taschereau monument, to the history of the Catholic Church, and so on. With the coming of the Tall Ships, the importance of the fleuve Saint-Laurent (St. Lawrence River) and its relation to the city will be thoroughly treated.

The use of different type makes it easy to distinguish between purely descriptive passages and general commentary.

In addition to this first circuit, there is a one-day excursion which allows the tourist to become acquainted with the different districts and the tourist and historical attractions of the surrounding areas. This short trip is centred on a visual knowledge of the sites and is much less detailed than the walking tour. The most important points of interest are indicated, and, once there, the visitor will be able to find much information about the different sites if he or she so desires.

An explicative text completes these two tours. It puts the history of the city into the perspective of the North American geopolitical context. It must be remembered that Québec City was once the capital of an empire "from which great explorers, with their guns on their shoulders and a song in their hearts, set out to establish a new France in America, stretching from Hudson's Bay to Louisiana and from rich Acadia to the foot of the Rocky Mountains."[2] Today, Québec City is still, in a way, the capital of French North America.

The different parts of this guidebook may be read separately, irrespective of the order in which they appear. Although this formula leads to a certain amount of repetition, we feel it has many advantages.

We would like to wish a pleasant stay to all the readers of this souvenir guidebook. We hope they will take back with them the same souvenir as this nineteenth-century American tourist. "Dear Old Québec, Good bye. I came to your gate a stranger. I came for ties of wood, and carry back ties more enduring than stone-ties of the heart. For every courtesy I thank you and assure you that as long as memory is vouchsafed me, so long will you hold a loving place in my inmost affection. Would that I might speak all I feel, but language is meagre and fails my wish. If you could read me my heart, you would know how hard it is to say — QUÉBEC — GOOD BYE".[3]

Jacques Cartier
(1491-1557)

Samuel de Champlain
(1570-1635)

Québec through the centuries

"Québec un fait de géographie." *(Raoul Blanchard)*
Québec City occupies a remarkable site. Located at the narrowing of the river where Cap Diamant rises to a height of about one hundred metres, the city has an outstanding harbour and an inland waterway, the rivière Saint-Charles, which the Amerindians called "Kabir Kouba", the river of a thousand windings. Jacques Cartier first christened this river "Sainte-Croix", but the Récollets later renamed it "rivière Saint-Charles" in honour of a benefactor. All the qualities of a site destined for a brilliant future were present at this location.

The motto of the city of Québec, "Gift of God, I will make thee worthy", recalls the magnificence of this site, which has been called a true gift of Nature. In 1949, the municipal authorities commissioned a report on the city's coat of arms following a suggestion made by the Société historique de Québec. According to the authors of this report, Champlain, one of whose ships bore the name "Gift of God", was to have been heard to exclaim "What gift of God is given to us here! But the unexploited riches do not suffice, lying fallow they remain barren. We must make them productive, exploit them, develop them."[1] Thus, Champlain's words were the inspiration for the city's motto.

The Amerindian Period
When the Europeans started to sail the seas in search of new lands, the site of Québec City had long since been occupied by the Amerindians. Their ancestors, hunters of mammoth and caribou, had come from Asia more than 40 000 years ago. At that time, Alaska was still joined to Siberia as a result of glaciation. Gradually, the new arrivals spread out over America, and at the time of the Europeans' arrival, there were more than 225 000 in Canada, of which close to 20 000 lived on territory belonging to, what is now, the Province of Québec. They had founded a large village by the name of Stadacona which was built on the heights of Cap Diamant. It was the capital of a small region, Canada, an Amerindian term meaning "village" or "small community". In the 17th century, Canada extended from about the Île d'Orléans to the Portneuf region, situated about sixty kilometres to the west of Québec. Along with other settlements in the St. Lawrence Valley, including Hochelaga (Montreal) which exercised a certain supremacy over all the peoples of the valley at that time, Stadacona (Quebec City) was an important Amerindian centre.

From Saint-Malo, Brittany, to Stadacona, Canada

Jacques Cartier was the first European to winter in the Québec City area. He set up camp there in 1535, during his second voyage to America. In 1534, during his first mission, the navigator from Saint-Malo had not sailed beyond Anticosti Island. At Québec City, Cartier set up his encampment at the confluence of the rivières Saint-Charles and Lairet, the latter of which has disappeared today. This first experience on Canadian soil was very difficult. Cartier lost several members of his crew due to scurvy.

This disease, caused by a lack of vitamin C, made its appearance in December 1535. The sick first suffered from general fatigue. The legs, hips, then shoulders became swollen. The mouth became "so infected and rotten at the gums that all the flesh fell from them, up to the roots of the teeth, which had almost all fallen out."[2]

The disease was kept hidden from the Amerindians. It was feared that they would take advantage of this very difficult period to attack the little colony. Cartier, by ordering his able-bodied men to double their efforts and work at several places in the encampment at the same time, succeeded in giving the impression that everything was normal inside the French camp. Through trickery, they obtained the long hoped-for remedy. An unsuspecting Amerindian interpreter, Domagaya, explained to Cartier how he had been cured of scurvy. Accompanied by two Amerindian women, designated by the interpreter, Cartier went into the forest to look for the precious remedy, the bark and leaves of the annedda, thuya occidentalis or white cedar, that then had to be boiled in "water; then, drink of the said water and put the mixture on the swollen and diseased legs."[3]

In spite of these difficulties, Cartier's second voyage to Canada remains a success. Cartier found neither the gold nor riches the had so hoped for; nor did he find a route to India. But he discovered a large river upon which he sailed up to Hochelaga (Montreal) and the realm of Canada. He also added to the geographical and hydrographical knowledge of the St. Lawrence Valley and became more familiar with the manners and customs of the Amerindian community and with the use of tobacco, which trouly impressed him. "They dry it (tobacco) in the sun," wrote Cartier, "and wear it around their necks, in a small animal skin, instead of a pouch, with a horn of stone or wood. Then, at any time, they make a powder of the said grass, and put it in one of the ends of the said horn, then put a hot coal on top, and suck on the other end, so that they fill their bodies with smoke, so much, that it comes out of the mouth and nostrils, like a chimney flue...." Cartier experimented with the "horn" and it seemed to him to contain "pepper powder."[4]

In 1541, Jacques Cartier came back to the Québec City area. He settled in the harbour at Cap-Rouge, which he named Charlesbourg-Royal and which Roberval rechristened France-Roy the following year.

Cartier's third expedition to America did not come under his command, but under Roberval's; moreover, the situation between the two men was not very clear. Cartier left for America without waiting for the expedition's head and returned to France even before Roberval arrived in Charlesbourg-Royal. Thinking he had discovered gold and precious stones, Cartier hastened his return. Meeting Roberval and the rest of the fleet in the Golfe du Saint-Laurent (Gulf of St. Lawrence), he continued on his way to France taking care not to reveal the contents of his precious cargo, which, alas, turned out to be only iron pyrites and quartz crystals, to the great disappointment of Canada's discoverer. Ever since, the expression "as fake as the diamonds of Canada" has survived, and the promontory of Québec City contains a "diamond" in name only (Cap Diamant).

After Jacques Cartier's voyages, France withdrew from the St. Lawrence Valley for some time. It did not, however, give up all hope of colonizing American soil. In 1555, Coligny tried to establish a French colony for his fellow Protestants in Brazil and, a little later, in Florida. But the Portuguese presence in Brazil, and that of the Spanish in Florida, prevented the French Protestants from making their dream come true. As for the settlements along the North American seaboard, they experienced a late start because of the severe climate and because they were not economically profitable.

Meanwhile, the cod-fishermen, who well before the acknowledged explorers had sailed the seas looking for the best shoals of fish, were the only ones to assure the French presence in America. Only in the 17th century did France think again of settling in the interior of the continent. Furs, which were becoming more and more fashionable, were to bring the French back for a second time.

The Founding of Québec

The opening of the fur trade, starting in the first quarter of the 17th century, constitutes without a doubt one of the most important events in North American history. Unlike fishing, which took place along the coastline, the fur trade would entail further penetration into the interior of the country and permanent occupancy of territory. The Amerindians, the principal suppliers, would undergo a complete change in life-style. Searching for new trading territory, the French would leave the development of the Atlantic coast in favour of the St. Lawrence Valley. They would go further and further inland. During the 17th century, the fleuve Saint-Laurent would again play an important role. It was not long before expeditions were organized.

In 1603, Samuel de Champlain was an observer with the Aymar de Chaste expedition led by Pont-Gravé. Arriving at Anticosti Island on May 20, they wasted no time in sailing up the fleuve Saint-Laurent. At Tadoussac, Champlain attended a "tabagie", a kind of fair with races, the exchanging of presents, songs, and dances. Champlain was not prepared for the spectacle that awaited him. The Algonquin women danced in the nude. Champlain described them as "well-shaped, plump, and dark-complexioned."[5]

Going around Île d'Orléans, Champlain, like Cartier before him, noticed and admired the falls to which he would give the name "Montmorency", at an unspecified date. Unimpressed by the site of Québec City, which he described in general terms, the explorer continued his journey upriver. Curiously enough, it was at Trois-Rivières (Three Rivers) that Champlain thought of founding the first settlement of the future colony. "It would be, in my estimation, a decent place to live, and it could be quickly fortified given its location and its proximity to a large lake."[6] Circumstance would have it that Champlain, five years later, would found the first Habitation at Québec City. The 1603 expedition then sailed up the fleuve Saint-Laurent to Hochelaga (Montreal) before returning to France.

In 1608, Champlain was entrusted with a new mission to found a new Habitation along the Laurentian waterway. This time, Champlain chose the site of Québec City, where he would arrive July 3, 1608. "No place," he wrote, "could be more suitable nor better situated than the point of Québec, so called by the "Savages", which is filled with walnut-trees."[7]

The virtues of the site were obvious. The harbour was excellent there. The promontory offered outstanding military possibilities. The rivière Saint-Charles, at a time when waterways were the only way to travel inland, would mean that the valley could be more easily populated. Lastly, starting at Cap Tourmente, situated a few kilometres east of the city, the shoreline of the river was flat and, therefore, easily inhabitable.

On arriving, Champlain had a first dwelling built at the

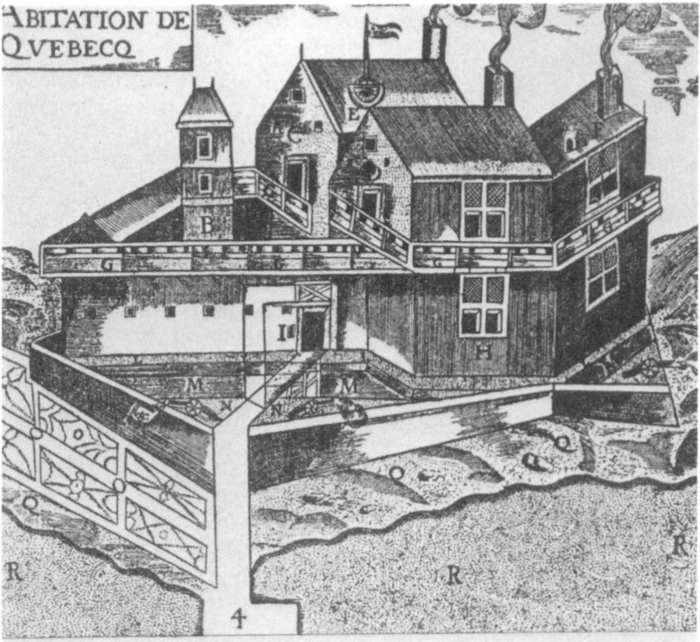

A Le magazin.
B Colombier.
C Corps de logis où font nos armes, & pour loger les ouuriers.
D Autre corps de logis pour ouuriers.
E Cadran.
F Autre corps de logis où eft la forge,& artifans logés.
G Galleries tout au tour des logemens.
H Logis du fieur de Champlain.
I La porte de l'habitation, où il y a pont-leuis.
L Promenoir autour de l'habitation contenant 10. pieds de large iufques fur le bort du foffé.
M Foffés tout autour de l'habitation.
N Plattes formes, en façon de tenailles pour mettre le canon.
O Iardin du fieur de Champlain.
P La cuifine.
Q Place deuant l'habitation fur le bort de la riuiere.
R La grande riuiere de fainct Lorens.

Gravure sur bois, d'après un dessin de Champlain, pour *Les voyages du Sieur de Champlain*, Paris, 1613.
Wood engraving, drawn by Champlain for *Les Voyages du Sieur de Champlain*, Paris, 1613.

Champlain's Habitation

bottom of the cliff where Place Royale is now situated. It was a kind of warehouse, residence, and small fort all in one. Very early on, difficulties arose. Champlain barely escaped from a plot to kill him and to hand the colony over to the Basques, with whom the founder of Québec had already quarrelled. Denounced, the instigator of the plot, Jean Duval, was condemned to be hanged. His "head was put on the end of a pike to be planted in the most conspicious spot of the fort."[8] And, like Cartier before him, Champlain had to contend with the severity of the Canadian winter. Out of twenty-eight winter residents, twenty died of scurvy.

Champlain, who still dreamed of discovering a route to India somewhere to the west of the great river, believed that Québec was destined for a brilliant future. A centre for the fur trade, a site for a colony, the stopping point for incoming ocean traffic, and the fortress of the St. Lawrence Valley — Québec would become the capital of the whole of New France, which, one day, would extend from Newfoundland to Hudson's Bay, from the Great Lakes to the Rockies, and from Ohio to Louisiana.

Nonetheless, the settlement progressed very slowly. In 1660, more than fifty years after its founding, the population of Québec only numbered some six hundred people of which about a hundred were monks or nuns. But, in 1681, the population of the town would exceed 1 300; in 1716, 2 000, and in 1760, 7 000.

The town acquired, from its outset, the physiognomy that it would retain afterwards. The religious institutions, the hospitals, the educational establishments, and the administrative or military buildings would be built in the Upper Town, leaving the business activities to the Lower Town where the Intendant, the colony's Superintendent of Finance, also built his residence and workplace.

Québec City: The Gibraltar of America

Already a political, economic, and religious capital, Québec also became an important element in the defence system of the St. Lawrence Valley. Situated at the narrowing of the river, formerly a stopping point for incoming vessels, Québec was the key element in this system. The taking of Québec was always the first objective of all the invaders of Canada, and there were attempts to lay siege to it on six different occasions.

In 1627, Champlain held out a first time against the Basques, but had to surrender the city two years later to the

British led by the Kirke brothers. Québec once again became a French possession in 1632 by the Treaty of St. Germain en Laye. In 1690, Frontenac resisted the attacks of Phips; in 1711, Walker, a large part of whose fleet had been stranded on the reefs of the Île-aux-Oeufs in the Golfe du Saint-Laurent, had to get back to his home port without attacking the town. In 1759, the English armies under the command of Wolfe defeated the French forces led by Montcalm and, in 1775, Carleton was able to ensure the defence of the town against the American generals Montgomery and Arnold.

Misunderstandings concerning fishing rights, border disputes, and the taking of certain strategic locations, such as Acadia, explain the numerous conflicts between the English and French colonies. These colonies were often on the verge of war even before their mother countries had declared the hostilities officially open. As for the American attack of 1775, it was a result of the War of Independence. The defeat of the French armies at the time of the Seven Years' War, in 1759, had especially grave consequences. Following the signing of the Treaty of Paris on January 10, 1763, New France became an English colony.

The first years of the new regime were particularly difficult. London wanted to govern its new colony according to the model established in its other North American colonies. Everyone who wanted to hold public office had to take the Test Oath in which one denied the basic principles of Roman Catholicism. This prevented Francophones, for the most part Catholics, from participating in the administration of the colony. The use of English laws and language and the desire of certain English merchants, denounced by Governor Murray, to benefit from the victory created a very tense atmosphere.

Following certain petitions and faced with the obviousness of the situation, London consented to a few modifications. The threat of a revolt in the thirteen American colonies led England to act in a more conciliatory manner toward its new Canadian subjects. In 1774, the Québec Act reestablished the use of the French language and of civil law, abolished the obligation to take the Test Oath, granted some rights to the Catholic Church, and considerably enlarged the territory belonging to the "Province of Québec" by extending its borders beyond the Great Lakes.

The citizens of Québec were satisfied with the new measures. As for the Americans, they saw in the Québec Act one more reason to revolt against England.

In 1775, they invaded Canada and laid siege to Québec. The resistance of the Québécois and the arrival of massive government reinforcements the following spring obliged the Americans to return home. The war ended with the signing of the Treaty of Paris in 1783.

The Loyalist invasion followed the military invasion. Some 42 000 Americans, preferring loyalty to the British Crown to independence, emigrated to the colonies which remained loyal to England. Thirty-five thousand people settled in the Atlantic provinces, six thousand in Upper Canada (Ontario), and a thousand in Lower Canada (Quebec). Their arrival led to a greater demographic balance between the English and French communities of Upper and Lower Canada. In 1791, Canada was divided into two provinces, Upper Canada (Ontario), almost exclusively Anglophone, and Lower Canada (Quebec), with its large Francophone majority.

Each province was granted its own institutions and its own government. Kingston was chosen as the capital of Upper Canada, and Québec became the capital of Lower Canada.

At the beginning of the 19th century, relations between the United States and England were once again strained. War broke out in 1812. The Treaty of Ghent put an end to it in 1814. But peace was still not assured, and England, believing that a conflict was still possible, decided to fortify Canada.

In Québec, important defence installations were undertaken. Around 1830, at the cost of some thirty-five million dollars, the present Citadel and other fortifications in the city were built. This defence system was finally completed at the end of the century and at the beginning of the 20th century, with other installations built in the area of Lévis, on the south shore of the Saint-Laurent. At that time, nothing was spared to make Québec the Gibraltar of America. The fortifications would, however, never be used. At the time of their completion, the danger of war between Canada and the United States had ceased to exist.

Québec: A Maritime Capital

During the last century, Québec was not only an important political capital and fortress located at a strategic point on the Laurentian waterway. It was also a maritime centre of world renown.

At the time of the Napoleonic Wars, France, unable to carry on hostilities across the English Channel, attempted to ruin England's economy by closing European ports to British ships. England got around this tactic by appealing to its colonies. Thus, a very active market was organized between Canada and its mother country. Once the war was over, England adhered to the principles of protectionism and continued to favour colonial over foreign products. Exchanges became more and more numerous until the middle of the century.

Québec benefited from this business. At that time, steam had not yet replaced the wind, and it was very difficult sailing upriver from the town. Going up the Saint-Laurent, from Québec to the interior of the country, and crossing the shallow expanses of Lac Saint-Pierre could sometimes take several weeks. Some sailors were so discouraged when faced with so many difficulties that they even unloaded their cargo before arriving at their destination. Québec became a stopping point for ocean shipping, the transit point between the sea and the continent. Canadian exports, mostly timber, left Québec, and most imported products arrived there from overseas. Thousands of people found jobs as stevedores.

The arrival of large numbers of immigrants constituted another important facet of the bustling activity of the port of Québec during the last century. Immigrants, many of whom were Irish driven from their island by famine, took advantage of the special rates offered by shipowners who needed to ballast their empty ships to faclitate the return trip to America. Between 1800 and 1850, some 30 000 immigrants arrived each year in Québec, often under extremely difficult conditions.

At the turn of the century, the demand for wood ships increased considerably. England needed to rebuilt its fleet after the American Revolution and the War of 1812. Québec, whose shipbuilding industry dated back to the French Régime, responded admirably to the demand and became one of the world's big shipbuilding centres. From 1 800 to the middle of the century, more than 1 500 ships were built in the Québec shipyards which were mostly located along the rivière Saint-Charles and at Anse du Cul-de-sac.

Economic development, linked mainly to maritime operations, had made Québec an important centre. On March 31, 1831, the House of Assembly of Lower Canada responded to a request of the city's middle class by passing the "Act to Incorporate the City of Québec". The bill, which received royal sanction on July 5, 1832, granted the city its first charter. It put an end to the system of Justices of the Peace and entrusted the administration of the city to a mayor and councillors elected by the citizens. The Charter was not renewed in 1836. The political situation of the time no doubt warranted this precaution. In 1841, Québec City was granted a new charter and went back to an elected administration.

Québec: A Political Capital

In addition to being the fortress of the St. Lawrence Valley, and a maritime centre of world renown, Québec has always been a very important political capital. At the time of the French Régime, the city had been the capital of New France. After the Conquest, when the colony became an English possession, the new military and political authorities were installed there. In 1791, when the Canadian colony was divided into two provinces, Québec was chosen as capital of Lower Canada. It would lose this title for only a few years at the time of the Act of Union but get it back again afterwards, alternating with Toronto until Ottawa was chosen as the new national capital. In 1867, Québec City became the capital of the Province of Québec.

The residents of Québec, who were very close to the administrative centres, were said to influence more than one decision. But the advantages of being the capital did not stop there. The economic activities of a city depended a great deal on the public service. The different governmental organizations in Metropolitan Québec now employ more than 40 000 workers. This relatively stable economic contribution, along with the fact that Québec City had long since been a stopping point for ocean shipping, considerably modified the city's vocation. It brought about a certain security which was the envy of more than one, especially of Montrealers. The latter, from the beginning of the French

Sillery Cove, circa 1870
(photographer unknown)

Régime, had had to depend mainly on their own resources to support themselves. The residents of Québec, on the contrary, because of the arrival of the ships, did not have to be excessively preoccupied with obtaining supplies.

A few years ago, the editoralist of an important magazine pointed out, no doubt with no malice intended, that "Montréal, oriented toward the hinterland and involved in communications, business, and conquest, resembled Toronto or Chicago more than Québec City, which was oriented toward sailing ships, originally carrying barrels of flour, and toward the orders and remuneration of public officials, and, above all, interested in nominations and promotions."[9]

An Important Turning Point

From the second half of the 19th century on, the continual expansion that Québec City had known for about fifty years stopped. The Canadian census of 1851 gave the population of Québec City as 42 000 and that of Montréal as 57 700. Fifty years later, in 1901, Québec City had only 68 000 citizens, whereas Montréal had 267 000. Different factors explain this change.

In the middle of the 19th century, England was faced with certain economic difficulties and with the certainty that the Canadian colonies would separate from their mother country as the United States had done. She abandoned her protectionist policies toward her colonies and adopted a system of free trade. In 1847, the laws favoring the sale of Canadian cereals on the British markets came to an end. Around 1870, the timber industry suffered the same fate; while in 1849, the laws governing navigation on the fleuve Saint-Laurent had already been abolished.

The closing of the British markets prompted the different Canadian colonies to join together and to seek new markets in the United States. The result was a certain continentalization of the North American economy in which central cities like Toronto and Montréal benefited more than eastern cities which, like Québec City, were too oriented toward the Atlantic.

The development of steamships and the advent of the canalization of the fleuve Saint-Laurent upriver from Québec moved the port of entry toward the centre of the country, and, thus, the city lost the benefits that it had derived from being at the heart of ocean shipping. Immigrants no longer arrived at the port of Québec, because the expected benefits were not to be found. The advent of a new maritime technology, based mainly on navigation by steam, and the demand for bigger and bigger ships, whose construction demanded large outlays of capital that only groups of builders belonging to monopolistic organizations could finance, would finally bring about the closing of the Québec shipyards.

In addition, the City of Québec was not able to take full advantage of the coming of the railway, the development of which was oriented toward the new economic axis of North America, from the second half of the 19th century on. The fleuve Saint-Laurent, which had contributed so much to the development of the city, thus became an obstacle. Different lines were built on the south shore of the river. Québec City, at a disadvantage because of its geographical position, would not really be linked to the railway until the Pont de Québec (Quebec Bridge) was built, in 1917, more than sixty years after Montréal was linked to the south shore.

Finally, with closer economic ties between the United States and Canada, the danger of war between the two powers was almost totally eliminated. As a result, Québec City became a useless fortress. In 1871, England, which was no longer interested in paying for the defence of colonies destined in any case to be separated from their mother country, repatriated its garrison. This caused a political and economic void which was difficult to fill.

From the second half of the 19th century on, the era of the great industrial and political barons was a thing of the past. Of course Québec City was chosen as the provincial capital in 1867, but this could not give the city the prestige and splendour that it had had in the era when it was the capital of a whole country. The provinces at the time of their creation were not important entities. Being a provincial capital could not put a stop to the decline of the city. Even the rapid expansion of the shoemaking industry at the end of the last century could not rejuvenate the area.

The Shoemaking Era

At the end of the last century, the shoemaking industry in Québec City underwent a certain expansion. The existence of tanneries and plenty of cheap labour, as well as advantageous customs policies, led some entrepreneurs to build shoe factories near the populous sections of Lower Town. "In 1878, about twenty shoe factories employed some 2 000 workers and produced more than 1 320 000 pairs of shoes annually".[10] "In 1891, the leather industry employed close to 4 000 people"[11], and "around 1930, more than 6 000."[12] In 1900, Québec City insured more than one-third of all shoe production in the province.

However, starting in the 1920's, the shoe industry gradually declined. The advantages of relatively low production costs no longer existed. Local provisions in hides remained insufficient. Quebec's policy of an agricultural sector centred on milk production limited the number of available hides. Added to this problem was the use of outmoded industrial techniques. The Québec City tanners were late in adopting the chrome tanning process. The industry's stockholders did not have enough capital. They were unsuccessful in lowering production costs enough to rival competitors in a market rapidly becoming saturated, especially after World War I. In the 1920's, the shoemaking industry was already on the decline. A series of strikes hastened its end.

The Great Fires

Starting in 1845, the history of Québec City was particularly marked by numerous and great fires. The Saint-Roch district, in Lower Town, and the Saint-Jean district, in Upper Town, were razed by flames in 1845. In 1866, the Saint-Roch and neighbouring Saint-Sauveur districts fell prey to the flames. In 1881, the Saint-Jean and Saint-Louis districts were destroyed. In 1889, the Saint-Sauveur area once again burned down. These fires affected the poor population most and struck staggering blows to the city's economy.

According to the newspaper Le Canadien, on May 28 and June 28, 1845, more than two-thirds of the city was consumed by flames. "The population of Québec City at the time of the 1844 census (the suburbs not included) was 32 876 people. Out of this number, the burnt-out sections of the city housed 20 157, divided as follows: 9 012 in the Saint-Jean district and 11 145 in the Saint-Roch district. The four other districs (Saint-Louis, du Palais, Saint-Pierre, and Champlain) together had only 12 719 people, or a little more than a third. And since the little that remained of the Saint-Roch and Saint-Jean districts equals what was destroyed in the Saint-Pierre district on May 28, it was not far from the truth to say that two-thirds of Québec City was in ashes. This terrible misfortune attracted many onlookers. And it was not an avid curiosity which brought them. No, it was an immense pity that guided these Montrealers to the port. There were a thousand of them on board the *"Sydenham"* and the *"Quebec"*, the latter vessel being the biggest and the most majestic ship to navigate on the river. They were taking advantage of the mild weather of July 7, breathing the fresh air, and being charitable. The destination was Québec City where the air still smelled of hot ashes and where the traveller could contemplate the chimneys, the half-walls, and the too-narrow streets of what had been Québec City. A thousand Montrealers left in the early morning to find out why the old city had burned. The captains promised a great show. The captain of the Sydenham, before docking, approached the Saint-Charles River so that his passengers could get a distant view of the sad ruins of the Saint-Roch and Saint-Jean districts.

"Our tourists took pity on the poor inhabitants. The sums paid out for their passage were used as relief funds for the residents of Québec City...."[13]

Further Along in History

Without attaining the importance that it had had at the time when it was the capital of Canada and a stopping point for ocean shipping, Québec City, in the 1940's and 1950's, underwent a new economic expansion. The growth of the civil service, the development of the tourist industry, and the effects of economic recovery all over the Province of Québec, particularly in the Québec City region, were the principal factors responsible for this growth.

In the 1930's, the different provincial governments, including that of Québec, were called upon to play an increasingly important political and economic role. Provincial jurisdictions, which were not very important at confederation, became much more so starting in these years. The demands of a society in constant evolution and the implications of the settlement of the 1929 crisis necessitated more government intervention. This was particularly true in Québec where many Québécois also counted on the government to give back control of the economy to the Francophone community. The nationalization of the hydroelectric industry, the foundation of the Caisse de Dépôt et de Placement (a government investment company), and the setting up of different state-owned companies during the Quiet Revolution also reveal a nationalistic tendency.

The increased importance of government activities was not without its influence on provincial and municipal budgets and on the hiring of civil servants. "In 1939, provincial and municipal expenditures were 192$ million; in 1945, 211$ million; in 1960, 1 160 000 000$, and, in 1965, 2 395 000 000$".[14] Nowadays, these expenditures exceed 30 billion dollars. "In the Metropolitan Québec City area alone, the number of jobs created by the different public sectors and for defence went from 18 196, in 1961, to 28 415, in 1971"[15] and to approximately 40 000 in 1980.

The development of the tourist industry constitutes another important element of the economic recovery that Québec City experienced starting in the 1940's. Beginning in the last century with the arrival of the Americans who made the trip from Niagara Falls to the chutes Montmorency, tourists have been coming in ever increasing numbers. In 1928, there were 500 000 tourists who visited the city.[16] In 1983, there were more "than a million to have spent at least 24 hours in Québec City. Of this number 506 871 came from the United States, 417 000 from the Province of Québec, 92 000 from elsewhere in Canada, and 12 488 from other countries. To this number can be added 84 796 people who attended congresses."[17]

Having again become a capital of some importance and benefiting from the rise of the tourist industry, Québec was also to benefit from the rapid industrialization that the province experienced starting in the 1940's. The strong wartime demand for industrial products brought about the development of new industries. In Québec City, 14 000 people found work in cartridge factories alone.

Finally, Québec City benefited from the economic importance of its own zone of influence. In order to respond to a regional demand which was becoming more and more urgent, the city had to increase the number of employees in the fields of education, religion, and administration as well as in the financial and commercial sectors. "Between 1951 and 1961, more than 15 000 jobs were created in Québec City in the social service, commercial, industrial, personnel, and public sectors, and close to 10 000 in the financial, business, and communication sectors".[18] In 1980, sales per capita in

The dirigible "R" 100 over Québec,
July 31, 1930
(Photo Edwards)

Québec City, assessed at 4 339$, was 20% higher than the Canadian average. The latter statistic well illustrates the city's role as a regional centre.[19]

Montréal and Québec City represent the two important focal points in the province, which is essentially divided into two large regions — Eastern Québec, dominated by Québec City, and Western Québec, centered around Montréal.

A north-south line drawn downstream from the city of Trois-Rivières, between the villages of Saint-Casimir and Sainte-Anne-de-la-Pérade on the north shore of the river and in the area of Victoriaville on the south shore, could be considered the dividing line between the two regions. Western Québec developed especially during and after the second half of the 19th century, and Eastern Québec during the years previous, when the port of Québec was the transit point for ocean shipping. Nowadays, the population within Montreal's sphere of influence is close to four million people, almost three times more than the region dominated by Québec City. Beyond these two large regions, there exist other distinctive regions which have been asserting themselves more and more during recent years. Given their small population and relatively weak political and economic strength, they cannot, however, claim to have escaped the influence of Québec and Montréal.

With the public service, which employs more than 40 000 people, the manufacturing sector, with more than 30 000 jobs (6 000 are in the food sector and 2 000 in printing works), the transportation sector with 14 000, and the financial sector, with more than 12 000 jobs, constitute the principal economic activity of the region.[20]

This recent economic development has changed the physiognomy of Québec City and the surrounding cities and towns. Ste-Foy, Charlesbourg, and Cap Rouge, which were still rural areas in the 1950's, have become large urban areas. Metropolitan Québec City now has more than 500 000 people, of which 175 000 live in Québec City. These changes have not always come about smoothly. The urban fabric of certain districts has undergone great changes, while other areas, such as that of the Gare du Palais (the train station), have practically disappeared, swept away by modernism.

Between the Sea and the Continent

The history of Québec City has always been intimately linked to that of the sea. The city is named after it. "Québec", in Amerindian, means "narrowing" of the waters or strait of the river. And it is precisely because of this geographical particularity that the site of Québec was noticed. Well-situated at the narrowing of the river, flanked by a steep hill, Québec, the cradle of French civilization on American soil, at once became the political, economic, and religious capital of New France. As the fortress of the St. Lawrence Valley, it was from Québec City that the French armies defended their empire.

The transit point between the sea and the continent, the city became a maritime centre with a world reputation in the 19th century. From Québec City, Canadian exports left for abroad, and imports arrived in Québec City. Between 1800 and 1850, more than a million immigrants landed in their adopted country at the port of Québec. Political capital and world shipbuilding centre, the city also became a maritime centre of great renown. And when the danger of war became more imminent, the British authorities decided to fortify the city and entrusted to it the defence of their American empire. Intimately linked to the world of the sea, the city experienced years of glory. Columnists wrote that it was the era when the city could compare itself favorably with any city in the world. In the last century, Québec City was "a little bit like New York in the summer, a little bit like St. Petersburg in the winter, and, all year round, a beautiful French provincial city transplanted onto British soil."[21]

Circumstances would soon change. The coming of free trade and of a maritime technology principally based on steam, combined with the effects of an unfortunate political crisis, led to a slow-down in the steady growth that the city had experienced since the beginning of the century. Between 1870 and 1930, Québec City entered a lethargic period which the even growth of the leather industry could not abate.

It was not until the middle of this century that the city was able to regain some of its importance. The development of the civil service, the rise of the tourist industry, and the effects of economic recovery all over the Province of Québec, especially in the areas immediately surrounding the city, were the principal reasons for this new activity.

Now, Québec City's importance goes beyond simple statistical data. It is the provincial capital, and some see it as the capital of the whole American Francophone community. Québec dates back to the beginning of the colony and has retained all of its history. Its archives, old squares, old homes, and numerous churches recall the different communities who have lived there. Its old walls and enclosures commemorate its former rivalries. Québec City, in spite of its growth, has remained a city of "walkable" size and has kept its charm and intimacy. It has also remained faithful to the river to which it owes so much. The magnificence and beauty of the heights of the city remain for us to admire. In 1984, a better site could not have been found for the gathering of the Tall Ships.

Footloose in Québec

The excursion through the streets of Québec is divided into two parts of approximately equal length and duration. Each part starts and ends at Place d'Armes. The itinerary includes about twenty stops. The reader is invited to pause at each location, which was chosen for its historical interest or for the panoramic view offered of the city, and to take the time to read the proposed commentary. The use of different type allows the reader to distinguish between strictly descriptive passages and general commentary. These stops, many of which are found in enchanting settings, will prove to be ideal sites for the tourist to find peace and quiet before undertaking the next stage of his or her outing.

The starting point for both parts of the excursion is the Champlain Monument, situated in Place d'Armes near the Château Frontenac.

Place d'Armes
(Photo H. Provost)

1 – *Champlain Monument*
2 – *Monument de la Foi*

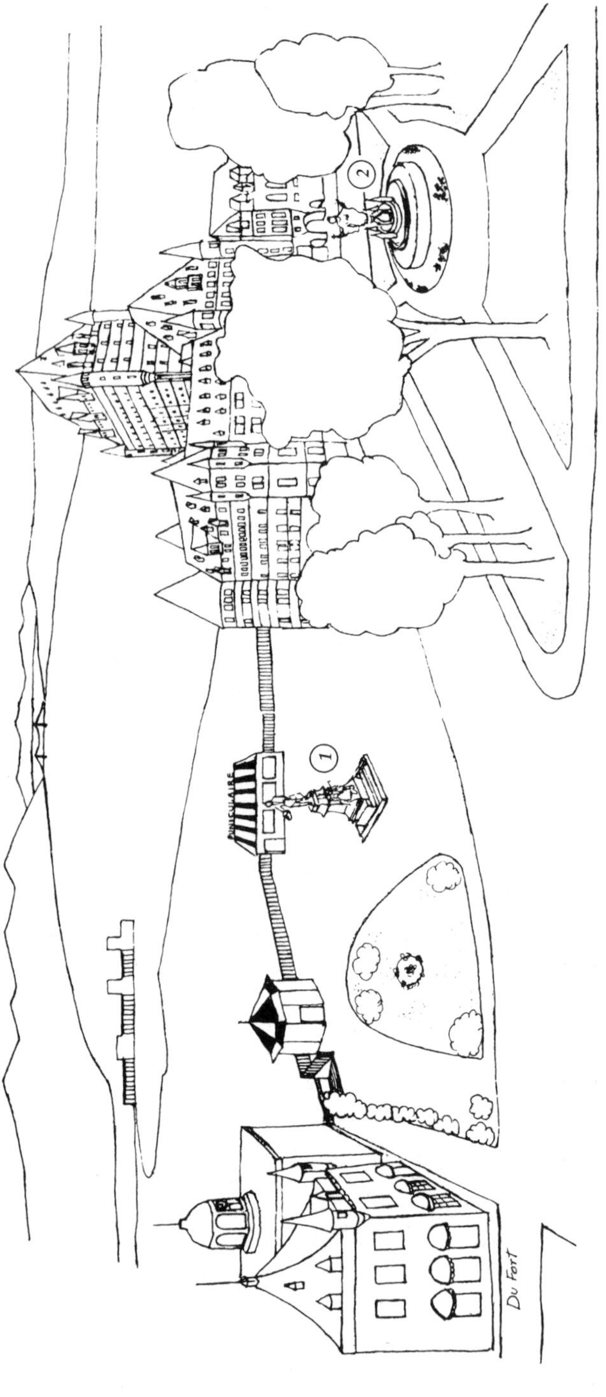

Place d'Armes

FOOTLOOSE IN QUÉBEC: First part

1. PLACE D'ARMES: AN HISTORICAL SITE

The Champlain Monument

The Champlain Monument was unveiled on September 21, 1898 by the Governor-General of Canada, Lord Aberdeen. It was the work of two French artists, Paul Chevré and Paul le Cardonel. The idea to erect a monument in memory of the founder of Québec was put forth by the Société Saint-Jean-Baptiste de Québec in 1890.

The base of the monument is made of granite from Vosges and the pedestal, of stone from Château-Landon, the same stone that was used in the construction of the Arc de Triomphe de l'Étoile and the basilica of Sacré-Coeur de Montmartre in Paris. The total height of the monument is about fifteen metres. Because there exists no authentic portrait of Champlain, the features on the bronze statue are not those of the city's founder but those of a rather unscrupulous auditor, Pariticelli d'Eméry.

According to the historian Lanctôt, "the bloated and weak character represented by the statue is an insult to the energetic and vigorous soldier and sailor" who was Champlain.

Samuel de Champlain was born in Brouage (Saintonge, France) in about 1570. The town registers prior to 1690 were destroyed by fire; as a result, we do not know Champlain's exact date of birth or the details of his baptism. When he arrived in New France, he was Catholic, but we do not know if he was baptized a Catholic or a Protestant.

Champlain received a pension as "royal geographer" from the French authorities.

In 1603, he was a member of the expedition led by Aymar de Chaste. They sailed up the fleuve Saint-Laurent (St. Lawrence River) in search of the best sites for a colony. Curiously, Champlain was indifferent to the beauty of the surroundings when they passed the natural harbour of Québec. His only remark was that the land would be as fertile as that of France, if it were cultivated. He found the location of Trois-Rivières more pleasing. He even thought of establishing a colony there. The group continued its way up the fleuve Saint-Laurent as far as Montréal, then returned home to France.

The next year, Champlain came back to America where he vainly tried to establish a colony in Acadia. The site was soon abandoned in favour of the fleuve Saint-Laurent. In the spring of 1608, Champlain took command of a new mission to New France with the purpose of founding settlements along the fleuve Saint-Laurent. On June 3, he arrived at Tadoussac where he was forced to fight a battle against a group of Basques — an ominous beginning which indicated that the occupation of the St. Lawrence Valley would not be all smooth sailing. When this conflict was settled, Champlain decided to leave his ship, Don de Dieu (Gift of God), at Tadoussac and to continue on up the river in a small boat. On July 3, 1608, the small group of men finally arrived at Québec.[7]

"From the Île d'Orléans to Québec," wrote Champlain, "there is a distance of one league, and I arrived on July 3. Immediately, I looked for a suitable location for our dwelling. The most convenient and the best situated of all was the point of Québec, thus called by the Savages. The site is full of walnut trees."[1]

Québec, the cradle of French civilization in America, occupies an exceptional site. Situated at the narrowing of the fleuve Saint-Laurent, Québec was the stopping point for incoming ships. During the period of sailing ships, it was difficult to continue upriver from Québec. The rivière Saint-Charles afforded an inland access; the promontory, about one hundred metres high, provided an excellent vantage point from which to defend the settlement.

Champlain devoted the rest of his life to the establishing of France in America. He spared no effort in trying to insure Paris's support of the new colony, he made the trip from Paris to Québec twelve times, or so. As a geographer, he travelled through the colony in search of new scientific data; as a politician and soldier, he signed the first agreements with the Amerindian tribes. This led to the establishment of the first trading routes and of the fur trade.

In 1618, Champlain sent the French authorities two reports summarizing his programme. He wrote that the duties collected at Québec on all the merchandise going to, or coming from, Asia would surpass those collected in France by at least ten times. (Champlain believed he would discover the route to the Orient somewhere to the west of the great river.) The profits to be made by using the "shorter" route to China would be substantial. Champlain estimated at some 5 400 000 pounds the annual revenues of the colony. In the valley of the rivière Saint-Charles, he proposed the establishment of a "city almost as large as St. Denis, which will be called Ludovica, God and the King willing."[2]

In 1610, when Champlain was about 40 years old, he

signed a marriage contract with a 12-year-old girl, Hélène Boullé. Because the young girl was not sexually mature, the contract stipulated that two years were to pass before the couple could live together. Champlain received three-quarters of the promised dowry upon the signature of the contract; this amount represented some precious financial help for his ventures. The bride-to-be was a Protestant but converted to Catholism. In 1620, Hélène Boullé accompanied her husband to New France where she rejoined her brother, Eustache, who had already been given important duties during Champain's absence. However, she found it very difficult to adapt to life in the colony. She returned to France in 1624, never to set foot again in America. At her husband's death in December 1635, she entered the Ursuline convent in Paris and took the veil under the name of Sister Hélène de Saint-Augustin.

The Château Saint-Louis and the Château Haldimand

In 1620, Champlain had the small Fort Saint-Louis built on the point of Cap Diamant very close to the present site of the funicular. Charles Huault de Montmagny, Champlain's successor, turned it into a stone fortress. The third governor of New France, Louis d'Aillesbout de Coulonge, put up the Château Saint-Louis on the original foundations. This first stone mansion was later redone and, then, replaced by a more spacious one. In 1784, Governor Haldimand began construction of a new official residence for the colonial authorities. This château, which was named Haldimand in honour of its builder, was situated on the present site of the Château Frontenac. The Château Saint-Louis then became an administrative building. In 1811, new repairs were done to the Château Saint-Louis, which was thereafter called Château-Neuf (New Château) while the more recent Château Haldimand was named Vieux Château (Old Château).

On January 23, 1834, the Château Saint-Louis was destroyed by fire. Its loss was irreplaceable. The building had witnessed many historical moments. It was there that Frontenac had received Phips's emissary during the 1690 siege of Québec. In the Château, Vaudreuil and Montcalm had laid down the plans for the defence of the colony at the time of the Conquest. The Château Haldimand was eventually used for some time as a teacher training school before it was torn down in 1892 to make way for the construction of the Château Frontenac. As well as serving as the Governor's Residence, the Château Saint-Louis and the Château Haldimand were also at the centre of Quebec's social life.

It is told that, on August 22, 1787, "a ball was given (at the Château Haldimand) in honour of young Prince William-Henry of Clarence, during which no one dared be seated out of respect for a prince of royal blood! The ball began at about five or six o'clock in the evening and lasted until after midnight."[3]

The Upper Town and the Lower Town

Québec City developed slowly. In 1660, there were only five to six hundred inhabitants. It was not until the King took charge of the colony in 1663 that the settlement really progressed.

However, right from its founding, the city acquired a physiognomy which it was to retain later. Commercial establishments, company warehouses and industries were concentrated in the Lower Town; and there as well was located the Palais de l'Intendant, the residence and workplace of the colony's superintendent of finance. The Upper Town, which could be reached by the Côte de la Montagne (Mountain Hill), even during the days of Champlain, contained the fortress, the Governor's residence, and religious and administrative establishments.

In 1684, Baron de la Hontan described the city as follows: "Québec is divided into the Upper and the Lower Town. The merchants live in the latter part because of the convenience of the port, along which they have built very lovely three-storey houses, in stone as hard as marble. The Upper Town is no less beautiful and no less populated. The Château is built on the highest point and commands from all sides. The Governors-General, who make their everyday residence in this Fort, are comfortably housed. Furthermore, it is the most beautiful and the most extensive view in the world."[4]

The Monument de la Foi (Monument to Faith)

The Monument de la Foi situated in the centre of Place d'Armes was erected in 1915 in memory of the Récollets, the first religious community to establish itself in the colony in 1615. The monument was the work of the firm Gaston Vennat of Montréal. This symbolic work, representing Faith, one of the three theological virtues, was cast in France. The granite structure is the work of the Laforce brothers, Québec City masons.

Place d'Armes

The history of Place d'Armes, once known as "Grande Place" ("Great Square") and "Rond de chaînes" ("Circle of

Chain"), is closely tied to the history of the city. Here, near Fort Saint-Louis, regimental parades and inspections took place. With the construction of the Citadel in the 1830's, Place d'Armes was no longer used for military purposes. From that time on, the troops paraded and were passed in review in parc de l'Esplanade, situated along rue D'Auteuil and nearer army headquarters.

Place d'Armes still remained a very popular site. A basin about twenty feet in diameter; was built. In the middle of it there was a column. At the top, a child held a big fish from which water spurted out, to the great surprise of all the children. Around the basin, poles joined by chains were put up; thus, the name "Rond de Chaînes". At the time when horseback riding was still in vogue, it was a matter of pride to parade around the "Rond de Chaînes".

On the occasion of Queen Victoria's jubilee in 1897, the architect Charles Baillairgé, Québec City's public works engineer, proposed the construction of a tower in Place d'Armes. "The tower would be 150 feet high and made of wrought iron so that it can be used for both civic festivities and public mourning. A small observation gallery, which could also be used for fireworks displays, would be on the top."[5] Unfortunately for the ingenious architect who made such a great contribution to the city's architecture, nothing ever became of the project. Once, he even had the idea of installing an aquarium under the terrace.

From Place d'Armes to Parc Montmorency

From Place d'Armes, you go to the foot of the monument to Georges-Étienne Cartier, situated in parc Montmorency. You can get there by taking rue du Fort (Fort Street) which used to lead from Côte de la Montagne to Fort Saint-Louis. Or, if you prefer, you can take the stairway and footbridge, the new porte Prescott, which allows you to cross Côte de la Montagne.

1 – *Laval Monument*
2 – *Cartier Monument*
3 – *Louis Hébert Monument*
4 – *Site of the first cemetary*

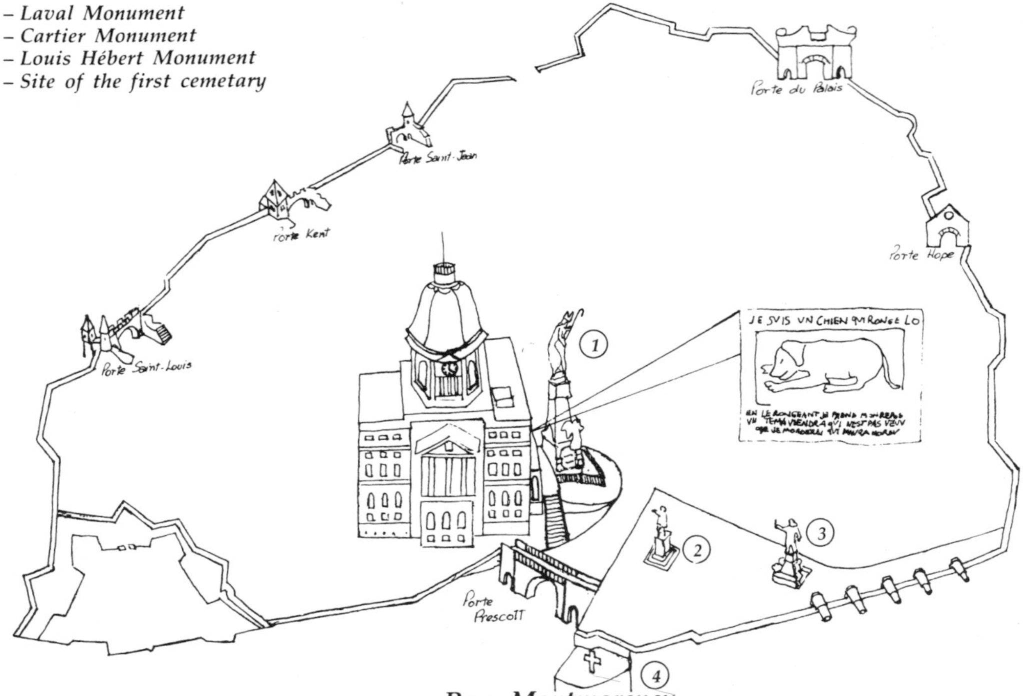

Parc Montmorency

2. PARC MONTMORENCY: THE HISTORY OF QUÉBEC — A POLITICAL, MILITARY, AND RELIGIOUS CAPITAL

The Cartier Monument

The Cartier Monument is the work of the sculptor G.H. Hill. It was unveiled to the general public on September 6, 1920 by the Honourable Alexandre Taschereau in the presence of a number of dignitaries, including His Eminence Cardinal Bégin.

Georges-Étienne Cartier was born in Saint-Antoine-sur-Richelieu on September 6, 1814. After having completed his classical studies at the Sulpicien College in Montréal, he was admitted to the bar in 1835. He was on the side of the Patriots during the 1837 Rebellion.

At that time, the political formation representing the Francophones was led by small industrialists and by some members of the liberal professions. Despite the fact they elected a majority of sitting members, they had no decisional power. The failure of the democratic process and the refusal of the ruling Anglophone minority in the colony to accede to the requests of the majority led some to an armed uprising in spite of the clergy's opposition. At first, there were sporadic encounters between government forces and the rebels; however, the situation rapidly transformed itself into a real confrontation. In the end, the Patriots lost, but the 1837 Rebellion led to the Act of Union.

In 1841, Upper (Ontario) and Lower (Québec) Canada were joined to form a single province, the United Province of Canada. Upper and Lower Canada had been formed by the Act of Constitution of 1791, which had also established the parliamentary system of government.

At the height of the rebellion, Cartier took part in the Battle of Saint-Denis but managed to slip away from the government troops and flee to the United States. He came back the following year after an amnesty had been declared.

Having cast aside his arms, he began to practise law. In 1848, he was elected a member of Parliament for the riding of Verchères and, thus, began his long political career. He became the leader of the Québec wing of the Conservative Party and the right-hand man of John A. Macdonald. Cartier was one of the most important architects of the Canadian Confederation in 1867.

In the second half of the 19th century, England was struggling with certain economic difficulties; as a result, she abandoned her protectionist policies toward the Canadian colony in favour of free trade. This change in policy forced the colonies to look elsewhere for help. The union of the different colonies seemed to be an interesting possibility. The creation of a united Canada appeared as the solution to ministerial instability and as the best way to secure the Canadian borders against American aggression and to develop an extensive rail system.

Without Cartier, Confederation would probably never have happened. As a reward for his marvellous accomplishments, Cartier was made a baronet and knighted. He died in London on May 20, 1873. On June 28, his remains arrived in Québec City where the people paid their last respects. They wanted to honour the memory of a great politician and a man of letters who composed some very beautiful songs including "O Canada, mon pays, mes amours." It was sung for the first time on June 24, 1834, at the banquet which led to the founding of the Société Saint-Jean-Baptiste.

Québec: The Political Capital

The Cartier Monument was built on the very site where the former episcopal palace had stood. This building had been put up at the request of Mgr. de Saint-Vallier in 1692. Throughout the years, it was remodelled several times and was the seat of the Legislative Assembly beginning in 1792.

During the French Régime (1534-1760), the colonial authorities occupied the Château Saint-Louis in Place D'Armes and the Palais de l'Intendant in the Lower Town. In 1763, the colony was given up to England. The new administration continued to use the Château Saint-Louis, but, because the position of Intendant disappeared, the palais was used for other purposes. The Château Haldimand was built in 1784 and replaced the Château Saint-Louis thereafter.

In 1791, England divided the colony into two provinces — Upper Canada (Ontario) and Lower Canada (Québec). Neward (Niagara-on-the-Lake), and later York (Toronto), were chosen as the capitals of the western province, and Québec was chosen the capital of Lower Canada. The choice of Québec was an obvious one. The city had been the colonial capital from the very beginning. On the eve of the nineteenth century, she was an important economic centre, stategically located at the dividing line between ocean and continental traffic.

In 1841, during the aftermath of the 1837 Rebellion, the Act of Union unified the two former provinces into one political entity. Kingston was chosen as the capital, but the choice was not unanimous. A compromise was proposed. Toronto and Québec City would alternate every four years as capitals of the new province. The compromise was rejected. In 1844, it was finally decided to move the Parliament from Kingston to Montréal where it met until the annexation crisis of 1849.

In 1849 some members of the English bourgeoisie were unhappy with the economic situation and with the adoption of the law granting financial compensation to the residents of Lower Canada who had suffered losses during the 1837 Rebellion. They set fire to the Parliament Building. The irony of it all is that, today, there is a fire station almost on the very same site as the burned-down Parliament.

After the annexation crisis, the system of alternating between Québec and Toronto was reverted to. In Québec City, Parliament would sit once again in the former episcopal palace located in parc Montmorency and reconstructed according to the plans of Baillairgé. In 1854, fire destroyed the building. The Convent of the Sisters of Charity on rue Richelieu was rented. Because this building had also just been damaged by fire, restoration work was begun immediately. Unfortunately, fire once again destroyed the building three months later. Parliament found a temporary home in the Music Academy on rue Saint-Louis and in the old Courthouse. Parliament was subsequently moved to Toronto in 1856.

In 1859, another building was put up on the site of the Parliament Building destroyed in 1854. This new building was used by the Members of Parliament in 1860 upon their return from Toronto. It was in this edifice that the Conference of Québec was held in 1864. At this conference, the framework was set for the British North America Act which led to the creation of Canada in 1867.

A painting of the Fathers of Confederation at the Québec Conference was done by Robert Harris. Unfortunately, it was destroyed during the fire in the Parliament Building in Ottawa in February 1916. The realization of this painting was, in large part, due to Wilfrid Laurier even though his party had opposed Confederation. Despite that fact, he supported the idea which had been put forth by the Royal Canadian Academy.

On the occasion of the Québec Conference, the city was in a festive mood. The highlight of the conference was undoubtedly the ball given by the Canadian government. It was held in the rooms occupied by Parliament; eight hundred and fifty people were present. A local newspaper claimed that, because of the ball, the merchants of Québec succeeded in "selling more gloves, flowers, ribbon, and lace than they will sell during the rest of the year" and that "the carters of the capital were made rich." What Prince Charles Edward had once said of the Congress of Vienna could well describe this conference — the Québec Conference didn't walk, it danced.[6]

Québec City lost its status as national capital on February 10, 1859, seen as a day of mourning by Québécois. From this date, Québec City became the country's old capital (la Vieille Capitale). In 1867, Québec City was chosen the provincial capital. Important as that may have been, the prestige and the glamour were not the same. Québec was no longer the capital of an empire.

Québec: The Fortified City

Québec City is located at the narrowing of the Saint-Laurent, a strategic location in the St. Lawrence Valley. The city has always had an important role in the defence of the country. Any sea invasion had to be beaten back at this point.

The first defences were simple stockades put up by Champlain. They were to protect the first dwellings built at the foot of the cliff. It was not until the year 1620 that it was decided to use the promontory. Fort Saint-Louis was built on the site and became the principal element in the defensive system of the city during the French Régime.

In 1690 following the attack by the English led by Phips, it was necessary to solidify the defences of the city. During the attack, a wall was hastily put up to protect the city. Obviously, such installations were inadequate. A few of the projects were carried out. For instance, an outer wall was built by Major Provost to replace the old entrenchments; and the Royal Battery was built and completed by the construction of the Dauphine and Vaudreuil Batteries in the Lower Town and the Saint-Louis and Clergy Batteries in the Upper Town. In 1693, construction of the redoubt on Cap-aux-Diamants was begun; it is found within the outer wall of the present-day Citadel. Other works were added to complete the first installations. These included the Cavalier du Moulin, the Dauphine Redoubt, the Saint-Roch, Royale and New barracks, as well as the powder magazines.

But, at the time of the Conquest in 1759, the fortifications were not yet very secure. There were no major changes following the Treaty of Paris in 1763. New France became an English colony, but the English seemed in no hurry to consolidate the defences of the town. At the beginning of 1780, landscaping work was done at the top of Cap-Diamant to make it easier to defend. In 1812, a new battery was installed, but it was not until the 1820's that Québec truly became a fortified town. At that time, the English authorities feared a new conflict with the United States.

The construction of the Citadel, the walls of the enclosures, and other defence installations were completed at a cost of 37 million dollars.

Six gates gave access to the town — the porte Hope located at the top of Côte de la Canoterie; the Saint-Jean and Saint-Louis, on the streets of the same name; the Prescott, at the top of Côte de la Montagne; the porte du Palais at the top of Côte du Palais; the porte Kent was built at the end of the 19th century on the site of a former postern, a sort of hidden exit inside an enclosure. Two more gates leading to the Citadel were also built — the porte Dalhousie and the iron-link gate.

These works were in addition to the four Martello towers that were built in a continous line to the west of the Citadel. Three of the four towers have been conserved. One is located on the Plains of Abraham, another at the corner of rues Laurier and Taché, and the third on rue Lavigueur. The fourth tower was demolished in 1900 to make way for the construction of the old Jeffrey Hale's Hospital on Boulevard Saint-Cyrille across from the Grand Théâtre de Québec. Four fortifications were built on the south shore of the river, three in the Lévis area at the end of the last century and the fourth at pointe de la Martinière, a few kilometres to the east, at the beginning of this century. Thus, the defence installations of the city were completed.

For both attackers and defenders, the heights of Lévis were of strategic importance. The story is often told of a young British officer on an exploratory mission in the Lévis area who knocked on the door of a humble cottage in the hope of finding something to eat. The farmer's wife was skeptical. "I hope you're not like the other British soldiers who left without paying." "Have no fear, madam," answered the officer. When he and his companions were refreshed, he held out a gold coin to the young woman. Rather than being happy at the sight of the money, she blurted out, "So, you're just like all the others. You don't expect me to have change for that!" One of the soldiers broke in. "Madam, you're talking to the PRINCE." "Even if you are the Prince, I have to tell you what I think" — Prince William Henry, the future King George IV, then spoke. "Very well, keep the gold coin. I'm giving it to you by way of compensation for the money owed you by those wretches who left without paying."[7]

The city's defences were never put to the test. Upon their completion, all danger of war had disappeared. The Treaty of Washington normalized the relations between England and the United States; as a result, Québec City became an unnecessary fortress. London called back its troops in 1871, and the Citadel of Québec was left to the safekeeping of a few Canadian soldiers.

With increased traffic in the city, it was decided to get rid of many of the fortifications built at great expense only a few years before. The porte Prescott disappeared in 1871, the porte Hope and du Palais in 1874, and the porte Saint-Jean in 1897. Lord Dufferin, Canada's Governor-General, wanted the city to keep its fortified look. He had the porte Kent built in 1879 and had the porte Saint-Louis enlarged the following year. The Porte Saint-Jean was rebuilt in 1939, and the Porte Prescott in 1983.

Québec: The Religious Capital

Because of Québec's political, economic, and military role at the beginning of the colony, it was only natural for the religious orders to set up their headquarters in the same place.

The diocese of Québec was established in 1674. At the time of the French Régime, it was the largest diocese in the world. The authority of the Bishop of Québec extended over a large part of North America, from the Atlantic to Louisiana. The changing political boundaries between Canada and the United States and Quebec's increasing population led to the division of the diocese. In 1956, the Vatican officially recognized the historical role of the Diocese of Québec by granting it the title of "Mother Church and Primatial Seat of Catholicism in Canada."

The Laval Monument

François de Laval (1623-1708), whose monument stands in front of the post office at the top of Côte de la Montagne, was the first Bishop of Québec. He was born in Montigny sur-Avre (Eure-et-Loire) on April 30, 1623. He was ordained in 1647 and was vicar apostolic of New France from 1658 to 1674 before being named Bishop of Québec. In 1688, he handed over his important and tiring duties to Mgr. de Saint-Vallier. Mgr. de Laval, or "Monseigneur l'ancien" as he was called, retired to Saint-Joachim a few kilometres from Québec. It is said he did this so as not to offend his

successor. He died on May 6, 1708 at the age of 75. His death followed complications from a chilblain on his foot contracted during the celebration of a church service.

He made a significant contribution to the development of the colony. He arrived in Québec just after the colony had been restructured from top to bottom and pacified thanks to the arrival of the Carrignan-Sallières Regiment. Québec was getting a new lease on life. Under the leadership of Mgr. de Laval, the church in New France would follow this lead. The founding of the Grand Séminaire in 1663 for the training of priests and the opening of a Petit Séminaire located north of parc Montmorency in 1668 were two of his main concerns. Public morality was another. There were numerous quarrels between the prelate and the civil authorities, none more heated than the one concerning the sale of alcohol to the Amerindians. The bishop clashed with the merchants who were supported by Intendant Talon. The latter considered that alcohol was an indispensible item in the fur trade. The question was finally resolved on March 24, 1679. Based on the opinions expressed by the Conseil Souverain de Nouvelle-France, made up mostly of merchants involved in the fur trade, by his confessor, Father La Chaise, and by the Archbishop of Paris, the King rendered an edict prohibiting the sale of alcohol anywhere but in French establishments. For all intents and purposes, this meant that it was business as usual.

The Laval Monument, the work of the sculptor Philippe Hébert, was unveiled in June 1908 on the occasion of the two hundredth anniversary of the ecclesiastic's death. That same year, Québec City celebrated its three hundredth (tricentennial) birthday. The monument dominates parc Montmorency named in memory of the first Bishop of Québec, François Montmorency de Laval. The name Montmorency was deleted at the time of his beatification in 1980 because its presence could not be justified by any contemporary documents.

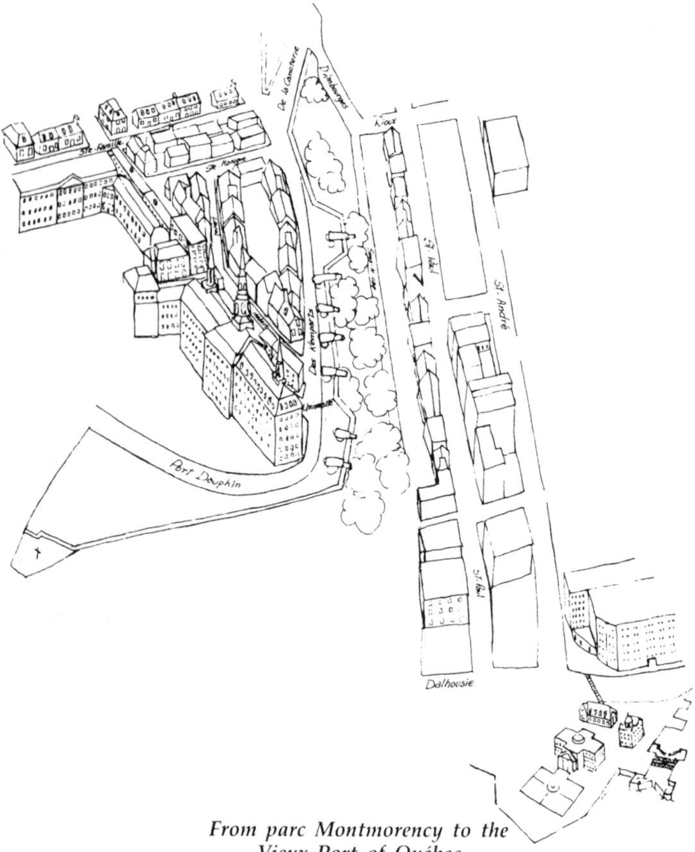

From parc Montmorency to the Vieux-Port of Québec

The Legend of the Chien d'or (Golden Dog)

On the front of the post office building located behind the Laval Monument, there is an interesting bas relief on which is engraved a quatrain in gold letters. The first line is written above a sculpture representing a dog lying down and gnawing at a bone; the other three are underneath.

"Je suis un chien qui ronge l'os
En le rongeant, je prends mon repos
Un temps viendra qui n'est pas venu
Que je mordray qui m'aura mordu."
(I'm a dog gnawing a bone
While I'm gnawing it, I'm resting.
There'll come a time not yet seen
When I'll bit he the one who once bit me.)

A member of the Québec bourgeoisie seems to have installed this bas relief on the front of his house built around 1735. Thereafter, this house served as a hotel and a post office before being torn down to make way for the present building upon which the enigmatic bas relief was installed. Many have tried their hand at an explanation.

Capitaine Knox, who arrived with Wolfe in 1759, proposed the following hypothesis. The dog, a symbol of loyalty, represented New France ready to fight for its King. The threatening lines were addressed to the Amerindians. Many other explanations have been put forth since that time, but most have been rather farfetched. The one that brought about the happiest result was the one told by William Kirby and which earned the author a great deal of fame.

In his novel *The Golden Dog*, Kirby speaks of the religious and economic disagreements Count Philibert had with the future intendant of New France, Bigot. Bigot obtained a royal decree from Louis XIV expulsing Philibert from France. The latter settled in Québec and became a prosperous merchant. A few years later, Bigot was named Intendant of New France. When the two former enemies met, the old hatred was rekindled. Philibert had the strange inscription placed on the front of his house. Bigot felt threatened and decided to use young Le Gardeur de Repentigny to eliminate his adversary. It is said that Bigot, Péan, and the latter's wife, Angélique de Méloizes, formed a villainous threesome.

He had just committed the crime when he recognized old Philibert, the father of Pierre Philibert, his sister Amélie's lover.

The tragedy put an end to the romance. La Gardeur de Repentigny gave himself up to the King's soldiers. Once freed, he came back to Québec and fought under Montcalm's orders. As for Pierre Philibert, the victim's son, he had no intention of taking his revenge. He understood that Le Gardeur never meant to kill his father. He still loved the beautiful Amélie who entered the Ursuline Convent to hide her grief. He died a bachelor at the Battle of Minden in Prussia.

The Site of the First Cemetary

A cross planted at the southern extremity of parc Montmorency indicates the location of the city's first cemetary. It is at this spot that the 20 companions of Champlain who died of scurvy during the first winter following the founding of Québec were buried. The cemetary of the Côte de la Montagne was the settlement's common graveyard until 1688.

The Louis Hébert Monument

Louis Hébert was the first settler in New France. Formerly, he farmed the land at the present site of parc Montmorency. Louis Hébert first settled in Acadia in 1604, but returned to France in 1610.

A friend, Samuel de Champlain, persuaded him to return to New France. Louis Hébert was an apothecary by trade, but he became a farmer and came to settle in Québec in 1617. He was the first Frenchman to live from the products of the land in spite of the rudimentary nature of the ploughing implements at that time. In fact, the first plough arrived in New France in 1828, one year after Louis Hébert's death caused by complications following a bad fall on the ice.

The Louis Hébert Monument, created by the sculptor Alfred Laliberté, is dedicated to the memory of the first settler in New France, to the members of his family, as well as to all the other pioneers of the colony. Unveiled on September 3, 1918, it was first put up on a piece of land next to the City Hall but later moved to parc Montmorency.

From Parc Montmorency to the Vieux-Port

To reach the Vieux-Port (Old Port) from parc Montmorency, you take rues Port Dauphin, des Remparts, and Université. The latter gets its name from the fact that the first French language Catholic university was located there. Université Laval was founded in 1852; it is now located in Sainte-Foy. The museum of the Séminaire is situated at 9 rue Université and should be visited.

VIEUX-PORT OF QUÉBEC OR QUÉBEC HE TIME OF THE SAILING SHIPS

The Project

The project to refurbish the Vieux-Port of Québec is the result of a federal government initiative. It aims at revitalizing the old maritime installations which have become outdated with the years. A lack of space and the necessity for a better road network led to the relocation of the port facilities downriver.

The project includes the building of a commercial centre with shops, markets, offices, restaurants, and cultural facilities which would include a museum of civilization built by the provincial government. A residential complex and sports centre, including a marina, will complete the renovation of the Vieux-Port of Québec.

The new installations are grouped around the old port facilities, quays, locks, and warehouses that dominate the Customs House, the National Ports Board building, and the pumping station parallel to the street. As a result, visitors will be able to relive the days of glory when Québec City played an important role in the maritime life of the fleuve Saint-Laurent.

The Customs House was built in 1856 according to the plans of Toronto architect William Thomas. It replaced the former Customs House built between 1830 and 1839 on the quai du Roi. The interior of this new building was destroyed by fire in 1864, and in 1909, fire destroyed the original dome which was replaced by the smaller one we see today.

Québec City at the Time of the Sailing Ships

Because of its location at the narrowing of the river, Québec assumed a very important maritime role early in its history. Incoming ships had to stop at Québec. During the French Régime, Québec was the only port and the only warehouse for all of Canada. A Swedish traveller, Pehr Kalm, wrote in 1794, "All exported merchandise leaves Québec... Everything coming from Europe and destined for Montréal or any other Canadian town must pass through Québec. When Montréal merchants return from trading furs with the Savages, at the end of August, they head downstream to Québec in September or October to sell their wares. Everything would lead one to believe that the Québec merchants were fabulously wealthy because of such a monopoly; howere, many people deny this ... It seems that they want to be dressed in the latest fashion and that their wives have their hair done every day as if they were being presented at Court. They eat, drink, and live well; each meal has many courses, etc.... To sum up, many are ruined by their extravagant behaviour."[8]

In the 18th century, furs were still the main export of New France. Thus, in 1739, out of export goods totalling 1 461 675 "livres" in value, furs made up 70% of this figure, agricultural products only 18%, fish 9%, iron from the St. Maurice Forges 1,3%, and wood only 0.5%.[9]

From the beginning of the colony to the middle of the 19th century, the port of Québec underwent a constant growth.

"Under the French Régime, the number of ships arriving varied form 4 to 20 year. From 1760 to 1785, the number increased frome 20 to 60. In 1795, 128 ships berthed in the port of Québec, and, in 1802, there were 211. From 1808 to 1819, arrivals increased from 334 to 630. In 1828, the number reached 701, and between 1830 and 1840, the average number of ships docking in Québec City was 1 000 annually."[10] The effects of the political climate at the beginning of the 19th century particularly favoured Québec. During the Napoleonic Wars, France was unable to cross the English Channel, but, on the strength of her powerful army, she undertook the closing of European ports to English ships. England got around this tactic by calling upon its colonies to help. After the war, England continued to favour its colonial market in the name of protectionism.

"In 1810, forest products formed ¾ of the Canadian exports. They had gradually replaced furs which counted for only 10% of exports in that same year. This compares with the figure of 50% in 1790, and 75% in 1765."[11]

Québec City, as Canada's principal port of entry, profited from this volume of trade. It became the debarkation point for thousands of immigrants arriving in America. "From 1829 to 1865, in the space of thirty-six years, no less than 1 084 765 immigrants landed at Québec City, an average of 29 300 a year."[12]

The effects of naval construction in full expansion in the first half of the 19th century added to the increased maritime traffic. In 1800, the demand for ships was extremely high. Countries were rebuilding their fleets decimated during the wars of the preceding years, and Québec shipbuilders answered the request. The salaries were relatively low, the materials were of good quality and sold at attractive prices, and, with a trade dating back to the French Régime, the shipbuilders knew what they were doing.

As a result, "the yearly average of 7 ships in 1800 increased to 13, then 18 in the following twenty years. Production reached 25 between 1821 and 1830, 42 between 1841 and 1850, 49 between 1851 and 1860... From 1792 to 1897, the Québec shipyards turned out 2 543 vessels... representing a total value of 55 million dollars."[13] At the busiest periods, about 5 000 people were employed. Of all the ships built in Québec, the most famous was undoubtedly the steamship "*Royal William*". Built in 1831, she was the first ship driven entirely by steam to cross the Atlantic.

A series of factors led to the decline of the port of Québec in the latter half of the 19th century. England abandoned protectionism in favour of free trade. A restructuring of the North American economy resulted. Cities, such as Toronto and Montréal, in the interior of the country, had an advantage over cities like Québec that were more oriented toward the Atlantic. The advent of steam power and the canalization of the fleuve Saint-Laurent made upriver communication much easier. Consequently, Québec City lost its geographical advantage.

These two factors were indispensible in the development of Montréal. It is not then surprising that the first steamship to provide service between Montréal and Québec City, *Accomodation*, was fitted out by a Montrealer, John Molson. On September 9, 1809, she made the voyage between the two cities in 36 hours.

The decline in the use of the port of Québec led indirectly to a decrease in other maritime activities. Fewer immigrants arrived in Québec City, and shipbuilders, unfamiliar with the new steel and steam technology, could not find the necessary materials in the area. Lacking sufficient financial resources, they abandoned production. In 1873, the Québec and Lévis shipyards employed only 800 men.

The history of the port of Québec also had its more social moments. The story is told of Horatio Nelson, the future hero of the Battle of Trafalgar, debarking in Québec at the end of the summer of 1782 and finding the great love of his life. The city has always had a reputation for welcoming its visitors. Captain Nelson was the object of extra special consideration. He finally fell head-over-heels in love with a young woman of extraordinary beauty, a certain Miss Simpson, whose parents owned a house on the Grande Allée. The day arrived when the captain had to return to sea. On the eve of his departure, he bid a touching farewell to the beautiful Miss Simpson. However, when night fell, his feelings got the best of him, and he returned to shore with the intention of deserting the navy. A companion, by the name of Davidson, was aware of Nelson's love affair and was waiting for him on the quay. Through persuasive arguments, some very forceful, Davidson succeeded in getting Nelson back on board ship. Nelson swore he would return, but he never did. He was unhappy in love but had a brilliant military career. He became the hero of all England. If it had not been for his friend, Davidson, England would have lost an outstanding admiral.

From the Vieux-Port to Place Royale

In order to get from the Vieux-Port to Place Royale, you can take the esplanade bordering the river; or, if you prefer, you can take rues Dalhousie, Saint-Jacques, and Saint-Pierre. At the corner of Saint-Pierre and Saint-Jacques, if you walk toward the cliff, you will come to rue Sault-au-Matelot. The street owes its name to the following incident. It seems that a drunken sailor jumped from the promontory to the street and thus gave the name Sault-au-Matelot (Sailor's Leap) to the site.

At the corner of rues Saint-Jacques and Sault-au-Matelot, there is a plaque recalling the defeat of the American, Benedict Arnold, at Québec on December 31, 1775.

During the American Revolution, Benedict Arnold suggested to General Washington that they attack Québec. The general approved. Despite numerous difficulties, Arnold led an army of a thousand men up the Kennebec and Chaudière Rivers and besieged Québec on November 13, 1775. Montgomery arrived at Montréal by the traditional Richelieu route and seized the city. He reached Québec in early December. A joint attack was planned for the 31st, the day before the contract of many of the American merceneries would expire. At the height of a snowstorm, Arnold from the east, and Montgomery from the west, attacked the Lower Town. The Americans were driven back. Montgomery was killed. Arnold continued the siege of the city until the following spring. The arrival of English ships, one of which was called Surprise, forced the Americans to return home.

The story is told that, at the time of the siege of Québec, some citizens of the town erected a wooden horse on top of the cliff, in full view of the enemy forces. They swore they would surrender only if the horse began eating hay.

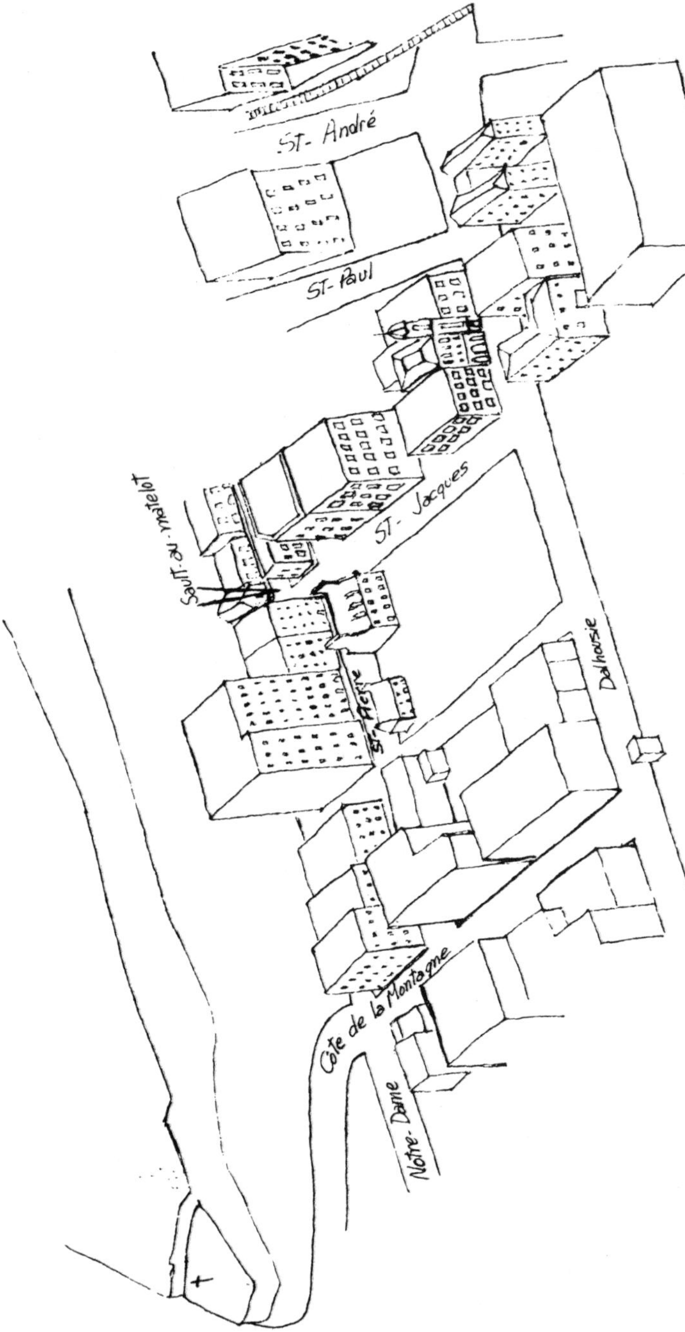

From the Vieux-Port to Place Royale

Québec vue du fleuve Saint-Laurent.
(Photo J. Boutet)

Rue des Remparts.
(Photo M. Beaudoin)

From rue Sault-au-Matelot, retrace your steps and take Street Saint-Pierre (rue), as far as Côte de la Montagne. Head in the direction of the cliff (turn right) as far as rue Notre-Dame. By following this street, you arrive at Notre-Dame des Victoires Church in Place Royale.

4. PLACE ROYALE: QUÉBEC'S FIRST MARKET

Place Royale: The Cradle of French Civilization in America

In 1967, the Government of Québec adopted a law aimed at promoting the restoration of Place Royale, a very important district in the history of Québec. This area is marked off by rue Dalhousie, Côte de la Montagne, and rue Champlain and by the cliff to the north.

Place Royale, the site of the first permanent settlement in New France, is the cradle of French civilization in America. Champlain built a first Habitation there in 1608; he then built a second one, much more spacious, in 1624. The Récollets built Quebec's first chapel at Place Royale the very year they arrived in New France, 1615. The consecration of New France to St. Joseph took place in this chapel in 1615. The building, which was situated to the west of Place Royale, was subsequently destroyed.

The first winters proved to be very difficult. The colony had to face many hardships, in particular, scurvy. In 1627, a company made up of London merchants financed an expedition led by David Kirke; its purpose was to drive the French out of the fleuve Saint-Laurent. Kirke seized Tadoussac and sent some Basque fishermen to Québec to demand the surrender of the settlement. Champlain resisted. Once again, in 1629, Champlain faced the Kirke brothers and was forced to hand over the town. This second siège took place in June, two months after the signing of a peace treaty between France and England. In spite of this, Charles II, the English monarch, refused to relinquish the conquered territories in America as long as his wife's dowry was not paid by his brother-in-law, the King of France. By 1632, everything was settled, and New France became, once again, a French colony.

In 1660, Place Royale was already densely populated, and its architecture resembled that of a medieval European city. There was a high concentration of houses, spread out along the narrow streets around a square that served as a market, a public square, meeting place, and execution site for criminals. The area was, above all, a commercial site. Merchants' houses and the store belonging to the Compagnie des Cent-Associés (Company of One Hundred Associates) dominated the site. There remains nothing of these first buildings; they were destroyed in the fire of 1682. The new buildings, built of stone from Beauport or from Pointe-aux-Trembles, were bigger and more spacious

than the first ones which had only a ground floor, a basement, and an attic and were made of wood or a combination of wood and stone, known as "half-timbering."

The Bust of Louis XIV

In 1686, at the request of Intendant de Champigny, a first bust of Louis XIV was installed in Place Royale. The idea did not meet with unanimous approval. The merchants of Place Royale claimed that the bust hindered traffic and had it removed three years after its installation. It is said that the bust was stored in the Palais de l'Intendant where it was lost when fire destroyed the building in 1713.

Between the years 1895 and 1931, a fountain was installed in the middle of Place Royale. It was demolished in 1931 and replaced by a second bust of Louis XIV which has also had an eventful history. It was a gift from France to Québec City in 1928, despite the reluctance of the French Consul General in Montréal. He feared that the gift, a reproduction of a work by Bervini, would offend the British; consequently, the second bust had still not been put up in 1930. The official reason for the delay was the high cost of the pedestal. Finally, the bust was set upon a much more modest pedestal in 1931. Numerous protests were raised, mainly by taxi owners. Once again, the monument was removed, not to be permanently returned to its place of honour until 1948.

The Conquest of Québec, 1759

Place Royale was completely burned to the ground during the War of Conquest. From July 12 to September 13, 1759, the English troops bombarded the city of Québec. More than 40 000 cannon balls and 10 000 bombs fell on the Lower Town. The area had been evacuated and the loss of life was low but material damages were beyond calculation.

In November 1759, Mgr. Pontbriand described the state of the city: "Québec was bombarded for two months; one hundred and eighty houses were burned by the fire bombs; all the rest were riddled by cannons and bombs. The six-foot thick walls were unable to withstand it; the vaults in which individuals had placed their belongings were burned, crushed and pulverized, during and after the siege."[14]

Place Royale in the 19th Century

In 1763, New France became an English colony and the commercial exchanges between Canada and England grew more and more frequent. Québec profited from the relationship. At the end of the 17th century, a hundred or so ships left the port of Québec annually; from 1800 to 1820, the number increased to more than 1 000.

Increased business and the arrival of ten to fifteen thousand sailors each year, however, did not have only beneficial effects. Taverns, inns, and brothels sprang up rapidly and led to the deterioration of the quarter. At that time, the most widely used garbage disposal system was the outgoing tide; at low tide, the shore would be littered with rubbish. In addition, ships' crews threw their refuse into the river which was also the main source of water for the Lower Town. The lack of drinkable water and sewers, the absence of medical care, and the poor sanitary conditions favoured the spread of epidemics. Immigrants crossing the Atlantic in wretched and unbelievably filthy conditions often arrived very sick at Québec. Cholera, the scourge of nineteenth-century Europe, spread throughout the St. Lawrence Valley. Québec was not spared. In 1832 alone, the disease claimed 3 451 victims. The curé of the basilique de Québec stated that "the city of Québec resembled an immense hospital, a sea of death.... The streets, the squares, the quays, and the shores offered a distressing scene of dead and dying."[15] The governments tried to avoid the worst. Protective measures were taken. Grosse Ile (Big Island) was turned into a quarantine site.

By 1850, Place Royale had already seen better days The reduction in maritime activity beginning in the mid-century only accelerated its decline.

Rich merchants kept their businesses in the Lower Town but built their homes elsewhere, particularly in the new, posh districts of the Upper Town.

Notre-Dame-des-Victoires Church

Notre-Dame-des-Victoires was built in 1688 at the request of Mgr. de Laval who wanted a church for the faithful of the Lower Town. It was put up on the exact spot where Champlain's Habitation had been located. A mark in the street indicates the precise location. The church was destroyed during the shelling of Québec in 1759. It was rebuilt in 1765 and restored in 1888 and again in 1929 on the occasion of the Marian Congress.

At first, the church was known as Enfant-Jésus (Infant Jesus); then Notre-Dame de la Victoire (Our Lady of Victory) in 1690 and Notre Dame des Victoires in 1711, following two French victories over the British armies.

In the 17th and, especially, the 18th centuries, the rivalry between France and England dominated international relations. The war spilled over into America where the colonies were already hotly disputing the best fishing and hunting territories.

In 1690, Admiral Phips, at the command of 34 ships with more than 2 000 soldiers on board, enjoined the Governor of New France, Frontenac, to surrender the colony. The British emissary received the following reply. "Go tell that pirate that I'm waiting for him and that I'll defend myself much better than he'll attack me."[16] According to Baron de la Hontan, if it had not been for the intervention of the Bishop and the Intendant, the emissary would have been hanged on the spot. Frontenac regarded the British fleet as a collection of disreputable pirates and brigands since he did not recognize the legitimacy of the new British king, William of Orange, who had taken the place of the ousted James II, a Catholic ally of France.

Phips twice attempted a landing. With the arrival of reinforcements, the French were able to hold him off. At the height of the hostilities, a French artilleryman succeeded in cutting in two, with one cannon shot, the mast on one of the ships from which flew the British flag; he, then, swam out and brought it back... so the story goes. At the end of October, Phips lifted the siege as he did not want to be caught in the winter ice. An exchange of prisoners took place. Louis Jolliet, the discoverer of the Mississippi, his wife, Claire-Françoise Bissot, and his mother-in-law, Marie Couillard, whose small boat had fallen into the hands of the British, were among those returned to the French.

The town's citizens, who had prayed to the Virgin Mary for help, renamed the church in the Lower Town Notre-Dame de la Victoire (Our Lady of Victory). Everyone believed that the victory was God's doing; He had interceded on their behalf. Mgr. de Laval believed it a true miracle when three French ships escaped from the British fleet moving downriver after withdrawing from Québec. The French were warned of the impending danger at Baie Saint-Paul and they tried to hide at the mouth of the riviére Saguenay. They were aided by a strong wind. Unfortunately, the British had spotted them and set off in pursuit, but the wind suddenly died down, and the British were unable to continue the chase despite five days' effort. The colony was saved. On board one of the French ships was 200 000 "livres" in cash.

In 1711, France and England renewed hostilities. Admiral Walker led a fleet of 98 ships and an army of 12 000 men up the fleuve Saint-Laurent. He was to meet with Nicholson who was at the head of a 2 000-man army entering the colony by way of Lake Champlain. The two were to join forces and capture Québec.

Once again, the population of Québec called upon the Virgin Mary to help them, and once again, She came to the rescue. Walker lost several ships and decided to turn back. When Nicholson received the news, he did the same thing.

From that day, Notre-Dame de la Victoire Church became "Notre-Dame-des-Victoires" (Our Lady of Victories). At the Québec Cathedral, on October 25, 1711, Joseph de la Colombière gave the same sermon he had pronounced, 21 years earlier on November 5, 1690, on the occasion of the French victory over Admiral Phips. His remarks went as follows:

"The Virgin Mary has saved Canada for fear that the sacrements be abolished. But, at the same time, She wants us to commit ourselves to put them to better use. This is the first part of my sermon.

"The Blessed Virgin has saved Canada because those who were attacking her intended to prevent the preaching of the True Faith. In addition, She wants Catholics to open their eyes and understand that they must profit from this sermon and not waste its message by the dissoluteness of public morality. This is the second part of my sermon."[17]

The priest was so inspired by the defeat of Phips that he not only composed this sermon, but he also composed songs and a hymn rejoicing over the retreat of the English. The first verse of the hymn goes as follows:

> "Ah, quel bonheur pour la Nouvelle France,
> On n'y craint plus les armes des Anglais,
> Le Ciel s'offense
> De leurs projets
> Et pour ne point exposer les Français,
> Il prend tout seul le soin de leur défense."
> "Oh! what joy for New France,
> We no longer fear British guns
> Heaven is offended
> By their designs
> And to protect the French from further danger,
> The Almighty, Himself, defends His followers."[18]

The Fires

Fire has been an everpresent danger throughout the history of Québec City.

On July 14, 1640, fire destroyed the Jesuit residence in the Upper Town along with Notre-Dame de Recouvrance Church, built by Champlain in 1632. On December 30 of the same year, fire broke out in the Ursuline Convent. The nun in charge of baking had a brilliant idea for keeping the leaven at the ideal temperature. She put lighted coals in the kneading-trough which was made of wood. Unfortunately, she went to bed and forgot to remove the coals. In 1682, fire destroyed the Lower Town. Only the house of M. Aubert de la Chesnaye was spared. The Annals of the Hôtel-Dieu de Québec report that "God undoubtedly preserved his property so that he could help his fellow citizens to rebuild their homes and businesses. He was a very rich merchant with a noble and generous heart. He emptied his coffers in order to lend money to everyone. There was almost no resident of the Lower Town that was not in his debt."[19] In 1686, another fire ravaged the Ursuline Convent. The Annals describe what happened. "This year on Sunday, October 20, it was Our Lord's will that fire once more visit our Community. We were all at Mass, and we had left the fires under control. As we were all at Communion, the alarm was sounded several times in succession. Strangers had come to inform us that our convent was on fire."[20] The fire had broken out in the kitchens of the institution.

In 1701 and 1705, fire destroyed the Séminaire de Québec. On January 5, 1713, the Intendant's residence burned down.

In order to protect themselves from future disasters and to avoid as much as possible damage caused by fire, a series of regulations and edicts was adopted. In 1727, Intendant Dupuy issued "an edict governing the Regulation concerning the construction of houses using non-combustible materials in the towns of the colony." The Intendant "forbad the use of wood as a building material in the towns. He ordered houses of two or more storeys to be built upon a permanent, vaulted cellar. He prohibited the building of mansard roofs. Double-sloped roofs were to be made of overlapping planks covered by slate or tile, and not cedar shingle, which was judged to be too dangerous. The Intendant suggested that the large frameworks be replaced by lighter structures which could be dismantled easily. He also suggested that gabled or partitioned walls be extended above the roofs to create a firewall to separate houses or sections of more important buildings. Chimneys had to be placed in stone partitions or isolated from any woodwork. The floor of attics or garrets

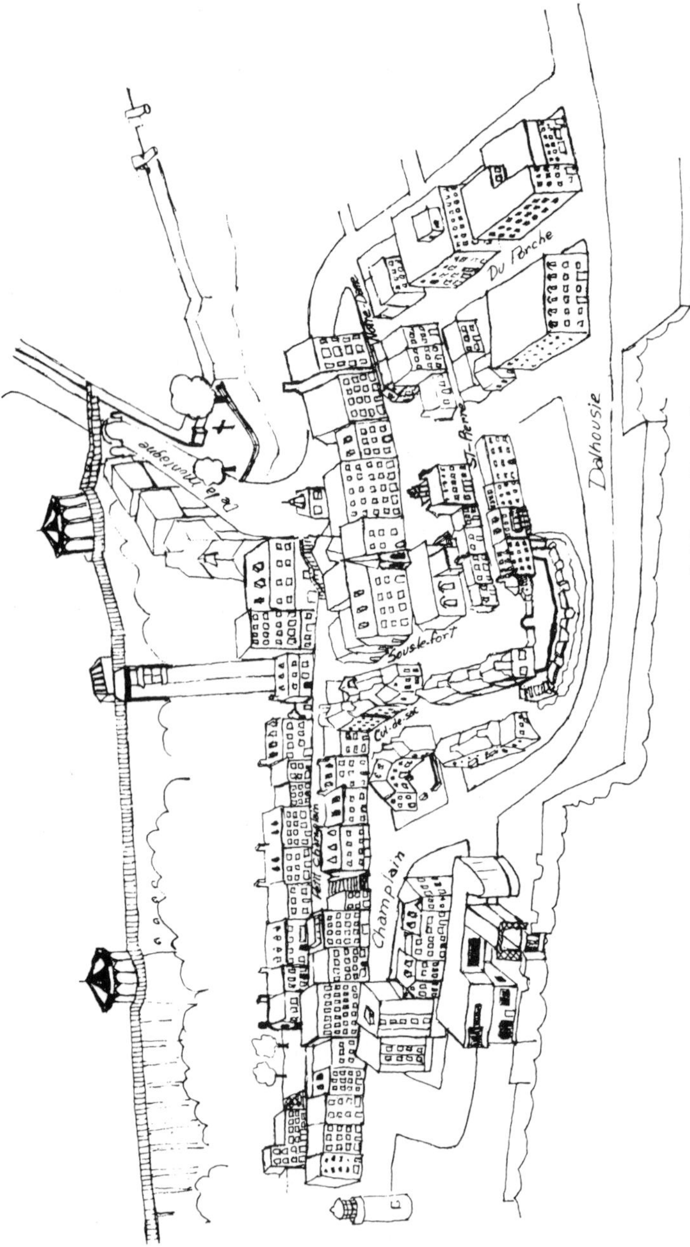

The tour of Place Royale

was to be covered with lime or sand to prevent a roof fire from communicating to the house. Finally, Dupuy forbad any visible woodpanelling on the outside of houses."[21] The building of Place Royale is an excellent example of the results of these regulations which provided a basis for a typically Québec-style architecture which developed during the first half of the 17th century.

Sightseeing in Place Royale

The basic principle underlying the refurbishing of Place Royale is not so much restoration as reconstruction. The area was literally reconstructed according to the fashion of the day, and often, with similar materials and techniques used at the time. As a result, the buildings can be analysed according to a single, historical perspective. Lacking are the makeshift additions found on many older buildings. The whole area becomes a huge museum, rather sterile in appearance. However, the overall beauty of the site certainly makes up for any of the disadvantages.

After a stop at the tourist bureau on rue Notre-Dame and at the Maison des vins (House of Wines), you return to rue Saint-Pierre where you will find the intrepretation centre. From there, you make your way to the Batterie Royale (Royal Battery), built in 1693 after Phips's siege of Québec. This makes for an interesting stop. Following that, you walk up rue Sous-le-Fort (Under the Fort Street), so named because it was situated directly under Fort Saint-Louis. After the second house, there is a passageway, but, before taking it, you should take the time to observe the mansard roofs of the houses on the street. At the end of the passageway, you turn right and head back toward rue Notre-Dame. Note the imperial roof of the turret of one of the houses. Back on Notre-Dame, you will notice the rounded corner of the house at the corner of rue Cul-de-Sac. This made it easier for the carts to turn the corner. Keep on Notre-Dame until you come to Maison Chevalier. Jean-Baptiste Chevalier, merchant, bought a piece of land in 1752 on which there were "walls lying in ruin." On the site, he had this two-storey house built. In 1763, Jean-Louis Frémont acquired it and turned it into an inn known as the "London Coffee House". In 1966, the Government of Québec purchased the house and began its restoration. It is open to the public and is often the site of exhibitions.

After leaving the Maison Chevalier, you get to rue du Petit Champlain by taking the stairway located to the left of 28 Champlain Boulevard. Before the landfill project, the river formed a cove which came right up to the foot of these

houses. At this site, called the "Cul-de-Sac" (Dead End), there were naval shipyards. Rue du Petit Champlain, built against the cliff, often had landslides.

As you walk up Petit Champlain, you will see the house of Louis Jolliet, the discoverer of the Mississippi. Born in Québec in 1645, Louis Jolliet began his classical education with the Jesuits. He received his Minor Orders at the age of 17. After a stay in France, he came back to the colony and, with Father Marquette, discovered the Mississippi. Louis Joliet was a geographer, an explorer, a businesman, and... an organist. It is said that he played the organ in the Québec Cathedral. His reputation went beyond the borders of New France. The British offered him a position several times, but to no avail. He had this house built in 1683 and lived there until his death in 1700. The house became the landing stage for the funicular to Dufferin Terrace in 1879.

From Place Royale to Dufferin Terrace

To get to Dufferin Terrace, across from the Château Frontenac, you can take the funicular which lets you off right there; or you can take the Champlain Stairs which American tourists call "Break Neck Steps". This stairway existed at the beginning of the colony and was indicated on the town plan of 1660.

We are led to believe that the inhabitants of the town did not exercise any restraint in taking their animals up or down the stairs. On February 22, 1698, the Conseil Souverain adopted the following police regulation:

"The council forbids any citizen of the Lower Town to take animals up or down the stairway which leads from the Upper to the Lower Town. Failing which, the violator will be subject to a fine."[22]

5. DUFFERIN TERRACE AND THE PROMENADE DES GOUVERNEURS: THE HISTORY OF A RIVER

A Commanding View

The Champlain stairs or the funicular lead to Dufferin Terrace. In 1838, Lord Durham, who had been instructed by the English authorities to investigate the political and economic situation in the Canadian colonies, had a terrace built on this spot. This first terrace, which was 50 metres long and 25 metres wide, was built on the actual foundations of the Château Saint-Louis, which had burned down in 1834. It was extended to its present dimensions, 425 metres, by the city in 1878. Lord Dufferin, Governor-General of Canada from 1872 to 1878, gave it his name.

The Promenade des Gouverneurs, inaugurated on September 9, 1960, completes the south-west extremity of Dufferin Terrace. The Promenade dominates the cliff, encircles the Citadel, and leads to the Plains of Abraham. The view from this walkway is truly magnificent.

The Discovery of the fleuve Saint-Laurent

The Amerindians called the fleuve Saint-Laurent "the river which walks", and the first Europeans to venture there, "the River of the Cod" or the "Great River".

There is no doubt that the Great River of Canada was known before the arrival of the official explorers of the St. Lawrence Valley. A century or two before the year 1000, the Celts from Ireland are said to have extended their domination to a land, known as "Great Ireland", which could be no other place than America. Around the year 1000, the Vikings occupied the Atlantic coast. In the year 1500, Newfoundland was Portuguese territory, and Miquel Corte-Real, a Portuguese explorer, and his companions most likely went up the Saint-Laurent. Long before the official discovery of the river, a great many fishermen from France, Spain, and Britanny exploited the rich banks of Newfoundland. Some went as far as the Saguenay. At the confluence of the Saguenay and the fleuve Saint-Laurent, the Basques had erected "chauffauds", a sort of fence on which they dried the cod, and they extracted whale blubber on the other side of the river, at Île aux Basques. At Forillon, a steep promontory between Cap des Rosiers and baie de Gaspé, the fishermen had built a small fort where at night they lit fires to attract the fish.

The official discovery of the fleuve Saint-Laurent is credited to Jacques Cartier who entered it during his second voyage to America in 1535. Having left Saint Malo on the 19th of May of that year, Cartier arrived in the gulf after a crossing which lasted more than fifty days. Near Natashquan, on the north shore of the gulf, he stopped in a small bay, now known as Sainte-Geneviève, but which the navigator named "Saint-Laurent", in honour of the saint whose feast day it happened to be (August 10). This name was soon extended to the whole gulf and then to the river. Cartier set out from the island of "l'Assomption" (Anticosti) and, following the directives of his Amerindian guides, discovered on August 15, 1535, "le chemin et commencement du grand fleuve de Hochelaga et chemin du Canada" (the route and beginning of the Great River of Hochelaga and the route of Canada). Continuing up the fleuve Saint-Laurent, Cartier reached Stadacona (Quebec), on September 7, 1535, where he spent the winter.

On the occasion of the Tercentenary of the landing of Jacques Cartier at Québec, a wooden cross was erected on the spot where the navigator wintered in 1535, now Cartier-Brébeuf Park. In 1889, 5 000 dollars was raised by popular subscription and a monument to the Jesuit martyrs was erected and a new cross was placed in front of this monument.

History is greatly indebted to Jacques Cartier. The navigator from Saint Malo noted that Newfoundland and Anticosti were islands and presented the first scientific notions of the river as far as Montréal (Hochelaga), thereby aiding later mapmakers like Champlain. The exploitation of the St. Lawrence Valley was to take place primarily after the beginning of the seventeenth century with the establishment of the fur trade as the main economic activity of New France.

"Crossing the Line" (The Baptismal Ceremony)

At the time of the first explorers, a special ceremony was reserved for those who entered the Grand Banks of Newfoundland for the first time, with the exception of those who had already crossed the equator.

"This ceremony", according to an eighteenth century voyager, "consists of disguising an old sailor in a big overcoat, a pair of boots, a white wig and a cap on his head, and large false white beard. Thus attired, the sailor comes down from the topsail where he dressed and, with the help of ropes and pullies, slides to the bottom of the foremast. Here, other sailors meet him and lead him to the foot of the mainmast where the initiate has been kept sitting on the edge of a large tub of water. Then Old Man Newfoundland makes the initiate swear that he will keep the secret from those who have not as yet entered this latitude and that he will never touch a sailor's wife, exacting the promise on the instant. If the initiate has not taken the precaution of offering money for a drink, he is immediately dunked into the bucket by the two men holding him; he gets out quickly and goes to change. During this time, Old Man Newfoundland goes back up to undress and leaves without the one who was dunked recognizing him. Thus ends this ceremony, which is far from pleasant in the cold season, and which is merely a sailor's game to get money."[23]

From Québec to Montréal

The river would remain for a long time the only route of communication between the different towns of the Saint-Laurent colony. The first land route joining Québec and Montréal, "le chemin du Roy", the King's Highway, was not laid out until 1730.

Depending on the winds and weather conditions, the length of the trip by river could vary considerably. In poor weather, it could take up to twenty days to cover the distance between Québec and Montréal. Travellers used the flat-bottomed boat. "There is no difference between the stern and the bow, which are both pointed. The sides are 4 feet high. Four or five benches, sometimes more, depending on the size of the boat, are placed abeam to seat the oarsmen. The boat is not greatly suited to sails or even to oars, but it is preferred to a boat with a keel for two reasons: first, because it draws less water, and second, because it is exposed to less danger on the lakes and rivers where strong winds are frequent." Passengers were protected from the heat of the sun and the whims of the weather by an awning of painted canvas which was raised in the centre and supported by hoops and which was large enough to cover half a dozen chairs and a table. Some boats had a mast suitable for carrying a sail, sometimes even a topsail. The boat owners took great care in decorating their vessels, which they considered a source of prestige. Travellers spoke with admiration of the intendant's boat which had benches all around, decorated with blue cushions, blue curtains on its sides, and which was covered with an awning of the same colour. All of the boats had a tarpaulin, or large canvas painted in oil, with which the awning was covered to give protection from the rain.

"In the eighteenth century, there were few inns to welcome travellers, and night was spent in the homes of the inhabitants. At times, the bad weather conditions made it impossible to respect the appointed schedule, and passengers had to sleep out in the open."[24]

The trip from Québec to Montréal was not made up only of annoyances. The view from the river was splendid, a point which all of the travellers noted.

The History of a City: The History of a River

The history of Québec is intimately linked with that of the river. Upriver from the city, navigation was perilous. Québec's natural harbour, well protected by the heights of Cap Diamant, was excellent. Thus the port of Québec became an important stopping-place along the Saint-Laurent. A maritime centre, political capital, and key element in the defence of the colony, Québec rapidly became prosperous and would remain so as long as these conditions prevailed.

From the second half of the nineteenth century onwards, the abandonment of protectionism in favour of free trade by the English authorities greatly modified trade between Canada and England. Relations between Canada and the United States normalized, and the United States gradually replaced England as Canada's principal economic partner. This gave rise to new economic structures more closely tied to the continent. This meant that the central cities like Toronto and Montréal were favoured to the detriment of eastern cities like Québec. The advent of the steam engine and the canalization of the fleuve Saint-Laurent facilitated navigation upstream from Québec and moved the terminal point of ocean navigation toward Montréal.

The different railway networks, which were set up from the second half of the nineteenth century on, followed the orientation of the new economic axis. As of 1859 and the opening of the Victoria Bridge, Montréal became directly connected to the networks which led to the United States. The city of Portland, Maine, became winter port to Montréal, and, in a certain sense, to the whole of Canada. In 1875, it is calculated that there were 1 024 miles of track in the Province of Québec, of which nine-tenths were on the south shore."[25] The River became an obstacle to the progress of the city.

A Bridge: A Necessity

For Québécois the need to unite their city to the new commercial centres under development had become urgent. In 1852, the engineer Edward Williams Sewell proposed to the mayor of Québec the construction of a suspension bridge over the fleuve Saint-Laurent. "Citizens of Québec", he wrote in his report, "you must build either a bridge or a new city.... Without the proper means of crossing the river, rival cities to Québec will rise up on the south shore and commerce will abandon the old capital."[26]

Québécois would have to wait until 1917, that is seventy years after the construction of the Victoria Bridge, before their city would be directly connected to the south shore. The construction of the Québec Bridge was not a priority for Canadian financiers, and it took a political decision from the federal government, under the leadership of Wilfrid Laurier, to ensure its undertaking.

Classified as one of engineering's masterpieces and ranked among the wonders of the world, the pont de Québec (Québec Bridge) remains today the longest cantilevered bridge in the world. It appeared in 1963 on a stamp issued by the Government of Honduras devoted to the large bridges of the world.

The construction of the pont de Québec was to take ten years. The first structure was poorly thought out, and, on August 29, 1907, it collapsed, taking seventy workers to their death. The Canadian Prime Minister, Wilfrid Laurier, declared shortly after the tragedy, "We must begin the task of making good our losses and continue the project." A new construction was undertaken.

Joachim Von Ribbentrop, the future Minister of Foreign Affairs of the Third Reich, worked as designer and inspector on the second bridge.

On September 11, 1916, the engineers decided to profit from high tide and to install the centre span. When it had been hoisted to a height of 6,71 metres, the southwest corner of the suspension span slid off its end supports into the river, killing thirteen workmen. Finally, a new span was hoisted into place on September 20, 1917, and successfully connected to two cantilever arms. The first train crossed the bridge on October 17, 1919, and the formal opening took place on August 22, 1919. In 1929, a roadway suitable for vehicles was added to the two tracks, and one of these tracks was removed in 1949 for the benefit of the roadway.

The pont de Québec, 988 metres long, with a distance of 549 metres centre to centre of the main piers, cost 25 million dollars. It is seven times the weight of the Eiffel Tower. This bulk, if converted into a girder weighing 30 pounds (14 kilograms) per linear foot, would reach some 1 288 km, that is to say the distance between Montréal and Halifax. The total weight of the structure, which is held together by 1 066 740 field rivets, is 59 862 tons.

The collapse of the pont de Québec gave rise to much commentary. It even inspired a poet, a citizen of the city, to compose the following patter entitled "On the Occasion of the Collapse of the Québec Bridge":

And it is you, my dear City
On which our misfortunes fall.
But what city, oh, my Homeland,
Has received more blessings from Heaven
Québec: Rome herself, Rome,
With her hills which man
Can never evoke or mention
Without pious transports,
With her unforgettable Tiber,
Rome has nothing comparable
To your immeasurable river,
To your rock, or to your port.
So, take heart! And, whatever happens,
Whatever destiny has in store for you,
Draped in your native grandeur,
Continue on your way without a murmur.
And of what consequence to you is this ordeal
From which our river still moans
Misfortune must rain
In the heart of a great city:
This is how God prepares it
For its sublime and rare role:
These blows, of which He is not sparing,
Will earn it immortality.

From the 1950's on, the pont de Québec was no longer able to meet the demands of traffic. In the autumn of 1961, the Québec government decided to build a new bridge. The bridge was begun in 1966 and inaugurated in 1970. The Québec government decided to change its name from Frontenac to Pierre Laporte to honour the memory of a Québec politician who died in historic and dramatic circumstances during the "October Crisis" of 1970. The construction of the Pont Pierre-Laporte was spread out over four years and entailed an outlay of 57 million dollars.

Crossing the River

Before the building of bridges, different means were used to cross the river. During the French Régime, canoes were used in the summer. These canoes were "made of birch bark and were about 20 feet long and 2 feet wide". They were "reinforced inside with ribs and very thin cedar strips, so that one man could carry it easily, even though this boat is capable of transporting four people and eight or nine hundred pounds of baggage. When you are inside one of these vessels, you are always, not within an inch of death, but within the thickness of five or six sheets of paper."[28] These fragile crafts were later replaced by wooden canoes.

The owners, canotiers, never refused a request, even if it meant crossing a herd of animals from the south shore to Québec. The poor animals were tied to the boat and had to swim across in the stifling heat, only to have their throats slit in the Québec abattoirs. If an animal weakened, its line was cut. If the owner wished to retrieve its carcass, he had to go to the Île d'Orleans or elsewhere.

The official ferry service between Québec and Levis was inaugurated in 1818, and the first ferry was the steamer "Lauzon". The horse boats appeared at the same time as the steamers. It was an ordinary boat, with a paddle wheel on each side; the paddle wheels were worked by a mechanism which was, in turn, powered by two or three horses which turned around a capstan. It was not unusual for a ferry boat worked by horses to be carried off course by the current and to take more than an hour to cross the river, or even to be swept along to the Île d'Orleans. They then had to wait for the next tide to return. Horse boats were abandoned around the year 1850.

With the arrival of the first ice, the steamers and other ferry boats had to give way to the canoemen, for the most part men from Levis, who handled the crossing in winter. Their canoes ("pirogues") were 25 to 30 feet (9 metres) long. They were cut from and hollowed out of the trunk of huge pine trees chosen with care and free of either knots or cracks. Both ends were turned up like the runners of a sleigh, and the bottom was slightly rounded and covered with a flat piece of hardwood nailed along its full length and used as a keel. Because of its shape, the canoe could glide rapidly through the water and readily be hauled onto an ice field."[29] The hardy canoemen worked extremely hard. The traditional canoe race, an important event of the Québec Winter Carnival, commemorates their feat. Nothing could stop them, nothing, that, is except the ice bridge.

The Ice Bridge

Depending on currents and weather conditions, the ice used to form a bridge almost every year; this bridge joined both shores of the river in front of Québec and brought a halt to

The ice bridge in front of Québec, shortly after 1879
(ASQ. Photo J.P. Vallée)

navigation. Father LeJeune was the first to mention this event in 1637. The last ice bridge dates back to 1924. The icebreakers prevent this phenomena from occurring. But here is how the bridge used to form:

In winter, the strait of the river narrows on each side leaving only a small passageway in the centre. The pieces of floating ice, carried by the tide, press against each other and form a dike which is the key of the bridge.

The bridge often formed at the end of December or January and remained fast until late spring. Its thickness could reach 12 metres. If, as it often happened, the bridge had not broken up by May 1, appropriate measures were taken. In winter, the bridge was a place for get-togethers and merry-making, a place for enjoying skating and sleigh-riding. Some people did a thriving business by installing "buvettes" or refreshment stalls on the bridge, an area which was for a long time free of legal jurisdiction. The bridge made everyone happy, everyone except the canotiers. Some experts submitted plans which would assure the formation of an ice bridge each year. Furthermore, stiff fines were imposed on those who were found guilty of breaking the ice bridge.

And so many other things...

The breaking-up of the ice bridge signaled the re-opening of maritime activity. From Montréal, the bundles of furs were once again shipped to Québec; and forest products, which constituted more than three-quarters of Canada's exports in the nineteenth century, were shipped from the forest area of the Ottawa River. Huge rafts, more than 12 metres long and 6 to 7 metres wide, were built out of beams. They often carried two rows of square timber which were floated as far as the port of Québec and then shipped to foreign markets. The rafts were guided by a crew, for the most part, of about fifteen men. Jos Montferrand was, without a doubt, one of the best known of the "cageux" or raftsmen. It is said that he knocked out the boxing champion of English Canada, in 1818, with a single punch. He has since become a legendary hero.

During the French Régime, eel and smelt had already made a name for Québec. Nowadays, eel fishing is carried out on a commercial scale while smelt fishing is done for sport.

The history of the river would be incomplete if we neglected to mention the legends which are associated with it and which are still alive in the memory of the people.

In 1542, Roberval abandoned his niece, Marguerite de Roberval, her lover and her old nurse, on an island in the gulf, known today as Île de la Demoiselle. At the death of her companions, Marguerite remained alone there for some time before being rescued by the crew of a French vessel.

Another legend relates that a Viking chief, Eric the Red, navigated the river as far as Montmagny.

In 1844, a solid ice bridge was formed between Cap Saint-Ignace and Île-aux-Grues, a unique event in the annals of the region.

On December 24, 1839. While hunting on the river, all of the male inhabitants of Trois-Pistoles were carried out towards the sea on an ice floe. The wind changed direction during the night and the men were able to get back to their village, by the grace of God.

The fleuve Saint-Laurent could tell us about so many things: the sailing-ship races opposite Québec in the last century, the many shipwrecks, the crossings, the history of the schooners, those wooden boats some 30 metres long with a tonnage of about 150, the presence of German submarines during the last World War, the history of the rail-ferries between Québec and Lévis.

From the Promenade des Gouverneurs to the Plains of Abraham

Continue walking west on the Promenade des Gouverneurs. At the end of the walkway, you have a magnificent view of the Plains of Abraham, offically known as Battlefields Park (parc des champs de bataille nationaux).

The Founder of the Séminaire:
François de Laval
(1623-1708)

1 – The Belvedere
2 – The Martello Towers
3 – The Citadel
4 – The Price Cannons
5 – The Wolfe Monument
6 – The Montcalm Monument
7 – The Croix du Sacrifice
8 – The Sir Georges Garneau Monument
9 – The Fountain
10 – The Water Reservoir

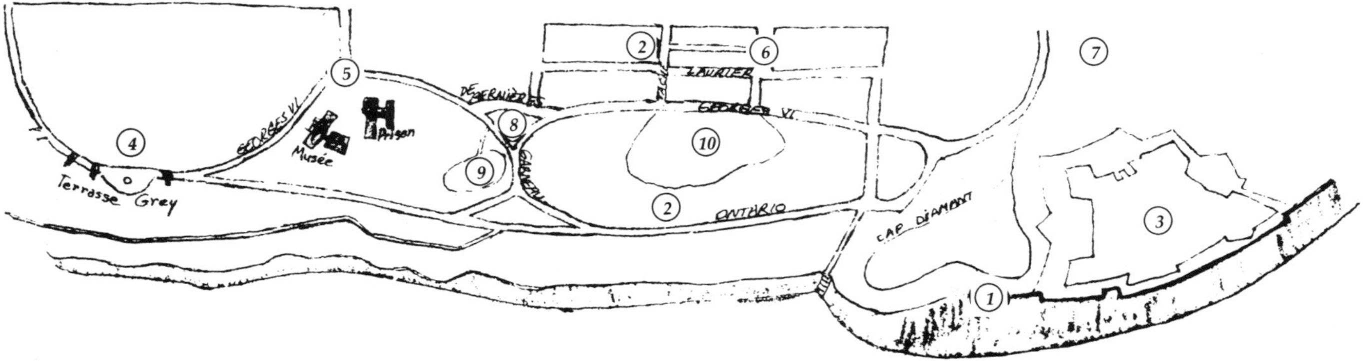

Battlefields Park

6. BATTLEFIELDS PARK: AN IMPORTANT STAKE

History

The idea of creating Battlefields Park originated with a work group set up to discuss the tercentenary celebrations of the founding of Québec. A federal law of 1908 created the Battlefields Commission and named its first members. Sir Georges Garneau, the mayor of Québec, was named president and remained so until May 1939.

A public subscription was organized to enable the Commission to obtain and exploit the necessary space. The first land acquisition dates back to July 22, 1908, when the city of Québec granted a site bordered on the north-west by chemin Saint-Louis and Grande-Allée, and on the south-east by the cliff. There would quickly follow other transactions involving the Séminaire de Québec in 1909, the Dominicans in 1910, and later the Québec and Canadian Governments, the Ladies' Protestant Home, the Ursulines and the city of Sillery. The last acquisition was made in 1954.

Battlefieds Park is often called the "Plains of Abraham". This name is very old and was used by English chroniclers of the Siege of Québec in 1759. The name is derived from that of Abraham Martin, who, in 1646, became the owner of a piece of land situated between rues Claire-Fontaine and Sainte-Geneviève. The name was later applied to all of the upper region of Québec. It is still used to refer to Battlefields Park, even though this was never part of the original property owned by Abraham Martin. The latter was a royal pilot and also the father of the second Canadian priest, abbé Charles-Amador Martin. (The first Canadian priest was Germain Morin, the son of Noël Morin and Hélène Desportes, widow of Guillaume Hébert).

The battle which brought about the capitulation of Québec in 1759, the victory of Lévis over Murray in 1760, and some of the military operations during the siege of Québec by the Americans in 1775-1776 took place on the "Plains of Abraham".

The Battle of the "Plains of Abraham"

Of all the events which have taken place on the "Plains of Abraham", the most important was, without any doubt, the confrontation on September 13, 1759, of the French and English armies. In the summer of 1759, England attempted, for the fifth time, the siege of Québec. After many years of war, New France was experiencing serious difficulties — her forts along the Great Lakes and in the region of the Richelieu Valley and Lake Champlain had been abandoned, and Louisbourg, the fortress of the Atlantic, had fallen in 1758.

On June 17, 1759, the English, with an army nine thousand strong and a fleet of fifty ships mounted with two thousand cannon, made their appearance before Québec. A first landing attempt east of the rivière Montmorency was thwarted. The English forces then took up position at Île d'Orleans and on the heights of Lévis. All summer long, the army continued its occupation of the surrounding villages and its bombardment of Québec.

During the night of September 12, four thousand men, led by General Wolfe, finally succeeded in reaching the heights of Québec by using a path situated near the actual site of Côte Gilmour, thus deceiving the French guards who were awaiting reinforcements.

General Montcalm, who had remained at Beauport, some kilometres east of the city, was immediately informed of the landing and quickly made his way to Québec. Although he had left fifteen hundred men at Beauport, Montcalm engaged battle without waiting for Bougainville's three thousand soldiers stationed at Cap-Rouge.

The English forces had taken up their position on a line running from what is now the old prison, situated near the Musée, to chemin Sainte-Foy. The French forces, about four thousand strong, occupied the site between the Martello towers Nos 1 and 2. The actual confrontation, which lasted less than an hour, took place in the vicinity of rue Cartier.

The French attack was poorly organized and lacked consultation between the French militiamen and the Canadian soldiers. Their lines were quickly disorganized. Once within musket range, the English fired a volley and stopped the French advance. Montcalm was fatally wounded and brought back within the city. The following day, after making the final arrangements for the end of the siege and the surrender of the city, he died, "Happy", he said, "not to see the English in Québec." The victor, General Wolfe, was no more fortunate for he too was mortally wounded. It is said

General Montcalm

General Wolfe

that when he learned of the victory of his compatriots, he exclaimed before dying: "I die content".

Deprived of its leaders, the French army withdrew a few kilometres outside of the city in order to reorganize. On Septembre 18, at the request of the citizens of Québec and on the advice of the remaining officers, de Ramezay, Commandant of Québec, capitulated. The news of the surrender of the city prevented the French forces stationed near Lévis from reopening hostilities. The next offensive was postponed until the following spring.

The Battle of Sainte-Foy

Lévis arrived at Saint-Augustin, some 15 kilometres west of Québec, on April 26, 1760, with more than 6 910 men. The next day, he approached the city and took up his position at the height of the Sillery woods, around the area of rue Joffre. A French soldier, who had been accidently carried by the current to Québec on a block of floating ice and who was discovered half frozen and half starved, told the English authorities of the French manoeuvre.

General Murray, Wolfe's successor, had at his disposition 3 866 men and a field artillery of twenty pieces of cannon and two howitzers. He occupied the strategic position of Butte-à-Nepveu, that held by Montcalm himself during the last confrontation. Murray decided to take the initiative. He ordered the artillery to fire on the French ranks, which immediately fell back to the Sillery woods. Murray believed that the French had retreated and ordered their pursuit. But Lévis and his troops engaged battle, in approximately the area of what is today rue des Braves. The French successfully circled around to the left of the English forces and thus obliged them to fall back toward the city.

This victory, France's last in America, would remain shortlived. The arrival of English reinforcements obliged Lévis to raise the siege and to fall back toward Montréal. Some months later, Vaudreuil would sign the capitulation of Montréal, bringing an end to the Seven Years' War in America. The Treaty of Paris, signed on February 1763, would finally put an end to conflict and make New France another English colony.

A French victory would have been surprising in the circumstances. France in those days was more interested in its European affairs than in America. The expression Voltaire used to describe New France, "quelques arpents de neige" (a few acres of snow), illustrates well the feeling which prevailed in the French court. On the other hand, the capture of Québec had remained one of the main preoccupations of England, no doubt urged on by its American colonies.

The supremacy of the English navy, the potential of British industry, and the disparity of the forces involved (New France, with its 60 000 inhabitants as opposed to more than a million and a half in the American Thirteen Colonies) all added to the advantages of England and made a French victory virtually impossible.

On the international level, the victory of the English forces solidified the supremacy which England was to enjoy for more than two centuries.

The American Invasion of 1775

In 1775, the city of Québec found itself once again under a state of siege. The Americans, who were seeking their independence, decided to attack the "Province of Québec", which had remained loyal to England.

Two armies were raised. The first, under the command of Benedict Arnold, set out from Cambridge and reached Lévis by way of the Kennebec and the Chaudière Rivers, a month and a half later. During the night of November 13, Arnold's small army managed to cross the river, to climb the same path Wolfe had scaled in 1759 and to reach the heights of Québec. Arnold advanced to within eight hundred steps of the city walls but, lacking artillery, was unable to cannonade the city. He then withdrew to a distance of some kilometres to await the arrival of Montgomery's army. Richard Montgomery had reached Montréal by way of Lake Champlain and the Richelieu and had managed to take the city. He joined Arnold's forces at Pointe-aux-Trembles on December 2, 1775.

On December 5, the Americans laid siege to Québec. All roads leading to the city were blocked and Québec was surrounded. However, the American batteries had little range and proved ineffective. On December 31, the Americans decided to storm the city for several reasons: they had few resources at their disposition; they could not count on starving the city, and also the mercenary contracts were on the point of expiring. The American plan was simple: two diversionary attacks, one in the direction of the Citadel and the other on porte Saint-Jean, would allow Montgomery's forces to descend Côte Gilmour, go along the river toward Près-de-ville (west of Place Royale) and then join Arnold's army coming from the Palais quarter (east of Place Royale). Their plan failed. The weather conditions were terrible. A

Carleton

heavy snow was falling on Québec. Montgomery, who had sworn that he would dine New Year's Day in Québec, was killed in the attack and his army was defeated. Arnold's army suffered the same fate at Sault-au-Matelot and was forced to withdraw to a distance of several kilometres from the city.

On May 6, 1776, English reinforcements arrived. Carleton sallied forth to disperse the enemy, thus ending the last siege Québec was to undergo. With Bourgogne in hot pursuit, the Americans abandoned Montréal, which had been an American city from December 1775 to the spring of 1776. The Americans had to return home having failed to turn Francophones against their new parent country.

Works, Monuments and Historical Remains

The National Battlefields Park has many buildings, monuments and other historical remains. Many of them are visible from the belvedere of the Promenade des Gouverneurs.

The Martello Towers

At the beginning of the nineteenth century, the colonial government continued to fear an American invasion. The construction of four Martello towers, a defense work which became more and more popular with the military, was commenced in 1805 and completed in 1823. At the time, more than two hundred Martello towers were built throughout the world, fifteen of them in Canada.

In Québec, the four Martello towers (of the eight which were planned for construction) form a continuous line of defense with the west side of the Citadel. Tower No I, built between 1805 and 1810, overhangs the cliff. Tower No II, built between 1809 and 1818, is situated on the highest point of Québec, on the corner of rue Taché and avenue Laurier. It served for some time as a museum. Tower No III, built in 1805, was demolished in 1905 to make way for the old Jeffery Hale's Hospital extension. Tower No IV, of which the construction was completed in 1823, is located on rue Lavigueur.

The word "Martello" is a deformation of "Mortella". In 1794, the English forces were impressed by the resistance of Mortella Point in Corsica, which was protected by one of these towers, and undertook the construction of this type of structure, of which the side facing the city was weaker. This meant that it could be demolished by cannonfire in the event that it fell into enemy hands. With time, "Mortella" became "Martello".

The Citadel

The Citadel, which dominates Cap Diamant, was built by the English under the direction of Lieutenant-Colonel E.W. Durnford. It was begun in 1820 and completed in 1831, at a cost of 35 million dollars. The English garrison occupied it until November 1871. Since 1920, it has been the headquarters of the Royal 22nd Regiment. The enclosure still preserves certain vestiges of the French Régime: The Redoubt of Cap Diamant (1693) and the old Powder Magazine (1750), occupied today by the Royal 22nd Regiment.

The Cannons

Of all of the cannons placed in the Plains of Abraham, the most important, at least from the point of view of their age, are probably the ten Price cannons, which face Grey Terrace and which were bequeathed to the Commission in May 1913 by William Price. One of these cannons comes from the French vessel *Le Prudent*, which was captured at Louisbourg, and another one was taken from Admiral Walker's fleet, which was wrecked on the reefs of Île-aux-Oeufs in 1711.

Grey Terrace

Built on one of the most picturesque spots of Battlefields Park, this terrace was dedicated to the Most Honourable Albert Henry George, 4th Earl Grey, Governor-General of Canada from 1904 to 1911. It dominates the cliff and overhangs the fleuve Saint-Laurent near Côte Gilmour.

The Prison

The construction of the prison of the Plains of Abraham began in 1860. The plans were by Charles Baillairgé. In 1871, it replaced the old prison on rue Saint-Stanislas. The building was abandoned in 1975 when a new prison was built in Orsainville.

The Musée du Québec (Québec Museum)

The idea of building a museum was launched in 1908 during Québec City's Tercentenary celebrations. The plans for the building, which was finally completed in 1933, were drafted by Wilfrid Lacroix.

The Wolfe Monument

Wolfe was buried in the small church of Greenwich on November 20, 1759. The following day, the British House of Commons adopted a resolution for the erection of a monument to the memory of the victor of the Plains of Abraham. Completed in 1772, the monument was officially unveiled on October 4, 1773, in St. Peter's College Church at New-Westminster.

In Québec, the first monument to Wolfe dates back to 1790. It was erected at the suggestion of Samuel Holland and stood on the spot where the general was said to have died. It served as a meridian marker. In 1832, it was replaced by another, in the form of a simple column, at the request of Lord Aylmer, the Governor-General of Canada. A new column was erected seventeen years later. It was restored in 1913, but it was destroyed in 1963 by the Front de Libération du Québec (The Québec Liberation Front), a terrorist organization devoted to the independance of Québec. It was decided on May 15, 1965, that the monument would be rebuilt.

Wolfe's Well

Wolfe's Well is located east of the Wolfe monument. It is reported that Wolfe, mortally wounded, wanted a drink and the soldiers who accompanied him drew water from this well. The well belonged to the Dominicans, who had it restored in 1931, and was acquired by the National Battlefields Commission in 1942.

Montcalm

There is no monument to Montcalm on the Plains of Abraham. However, a stele was erected between the Martello towers Nos I and II. It bears the inscription: "Montcalm, four times victorious, once beaten, always for the honour in arms of France, mortally wounded here on September 13, 1759."

Outside of the Plains of Abraham, there are many monuments, statues and steles which recall the French general to the citizens of Québec. The most important is the monument in parc Montcalm. It is a replica of the one at Candiac, France, and was a gift from France in 1911.

The Monument des Braves

On February 27, 1855, the Société Saint-Jean-Baptiste de Québec set up a committee to see to the erection of a monument to the memory of those who fell at the Battle of Sainte-Foy in April 1760. The laying of the first stone was to have taken place on June 25, 1855. However, the news of the imminent arrival of *La Capricieuse*, the first French ship to travel up the fleuve Saint-Laurent since the Conquest, caused the ceremony to be postponed until July 18 so that the ship's captain could attend. Later, a pedestal and a column were erected. Prince Jérôme Napoléon, on the request of the Société, made the gift of a statue of Bellona, the Roman goddess of war. This monument was erected on the former site of the Dumont mill where the English and French forces had fought on April 28, 1760. It was officially inaugurated on October 19, 1863. The National Battlefields Commission acquired it in 1908. Its small park became an outlying annex to the actuel Battlefields Park.

The Croix du Sacrifice (Cross of Sacrifice)

The Croix du Sacrifice was unveiled July 1, 1924, in honour of some 60 000 Canadians who died on the battlefield during the First World War. A handful of earth from Vimy, where the Canadians won renown, was deposited on the site. On November 9, 1947, Cardinal Gerlier presented to the Canadian Government soil from Alsace to be laid there in recognition of the aid provided by Canada during the Second World War. A commemorative service is held there each year on November 11, Armistice Day. It was suspended from 1939 to 1945 during the war.

The Sir Georges Garneau Monument

A monument dedicated to the memory of Sir Georges Garneau was erected on Avenue Wolfe on September 7, 1957. Garneau, who died in 1944, was a former mayor of Québec and the first president of the National Battlefields Commission.

The Jeanne d'Arc (Joan of Arc) Monument

This monument, an equestrian statue, was unveiled on September 1, 1938. It was an anonymous gift of two citizens of New York in memory of the soldiers who died in 1759 during the battle of the Plains of Abraham. (The doners were Mr. and Mrs. Huntington. Mrs. Huntington was herself a sculptress.)

The Fontaine du Centenaire (Centenary Fountain)

In commemoration of the centenary of Canadian Confederation (1867), for which the foundations had been laid at the

Québec Conference, a fountain was erected and officialy inaugurated on October 30, 1967. The spot on which it stands was formally the site of the buildings of the Québec Observatory, demolished after their acquisition by the National Battlefields Commission.

A Factory on the Plains of Abraham

Formerly, some buildings of the Ross Rifle and laboratories of the Arsenal occupied a piece of land west of the Citadel between the Martello towers Nos I and II. The Martello tower No I served as a base for the water reservoir of the Ross Rifle. These buildings were demolished around 1936.

Military Huts

In August 1939, the Ministry of National Defense obtained permission to build military huts on the Plains of Abraham to billet soldiers and their families. They were also used in a probably somewhat extreme security measure to lodge German Canadians whose liberty was restricted during the last war. The huts were demolished in 1951.

Québec City's Water Reservoir

The idea of building an underground water reservoir on the Plains of Abraham was conceived after the fire of 1899 in the Jacques-Cartier Parish during which the firemen had great difficulty with the water pressure. To get round this sort of problem, the city of Québec obtained permission from the Commission to build a water reservoir near the site of the former Ross Rifle buildings.

The First Performance of the National Anthem: "O Canada"

The anthem *O Canada* was performed for the first time during the Saint-Jean-Baptiste celebrations of June 24, 1880, during which representatives of all of the French-speaking Catholics of North America gathered on the Plains. The song composed for the occasion later became the National Anthem of Canada. The words were composed (in French) by A.-B. Routhier and the music by Calixa Lavallée.

The First National Eucharistic Congress

The first National Eucharistic Congress was held on the Plains from June 22 to June 26, 1938, and was attended by more than 100 000 people. A pontifical mass was celebrated by Monseignor Mark Duke, Archibishop of Vancouver, in the presence of Cardinal legate J.M. Rodrigue Villeneuve, Archibishop of Québec and fifty-five archibishops and bishops and 2 500 priests. On June 23, a midnight mass was celebrated and 150 priests administered the sacrament to more than 65 000 communicants. A repository altar, 40 metres high, had been erected. The carillon from the congress was later installed in the tower of the church at Boischatel.

The history of the Plains of Abraham has always been closely linked with that of the city. A privileged spot in history and one of the most enchanting sites, the Plains of Abraham have inspired more than one poet. In 1898, Willison McTennair devoted a poem to it; his work was later translated by Louis Fréchette.

Plains of Abraham

...
Montcalm and Wolfe! their glory such,
And such the outcome of their strife
That, under War's transmuting touch,
A new-born Nation leaped to life.
...
Their shades cry to us from its sod
To guard inviolate their dust; —
They died for Country, King and God!
Shall we prove faithless to our trust?

From the Promenade des Gouverneurs to the Jardin des Gouverneurs

From the Promenade des Gouverneurs retrace your steps back toward the Jardin des Gouverneurs (The Governors' Garden) situated to the west of the Château Frontenac.

The Jardin des Gouverneurs

7. THE JARDIN DES GOUVERNEURS: REMEMBRANCES OF FRANCE, ENGLAND AND THE UNITED STATES

The jardin des Gouverneurs has been in existence since the construction of the Château Saint-Louis in 1647. It was reserved for a long time for the use of the governors but became a public park in 1892.

The Château Frontenac

The plans for the Château Frontenac were drawn up by Bruce Price, a New York architect, and its construction was undertaken in 1892. It was enlarged in 1924 when the central tower, seventeen stories high, was added.

Owned by the Canadian Pacific Railway, the Château Frontenac is certainly the best known of all of the buildings in the city of Québec. With its turrets and keeps, it gives the city an air of olden times which recalls the towns that men like Champlain, Frontenac, and Laval left to come and build a new country in New France. Presently, the hotel has 660 rooms.

The Château Frontenac was built partly on the site of the old Château Haldimand which served as a governors' residence for the colony between the years 1784 and 1860. Behind the Château Haldimand stood the Château Saint-Louis, the first governors' residence in New France. This building was unfortunately destroyed by fire, in 1834. A stone from this old château was placed over the porte cochère of the Château Frontenac inside the main courtyard.

This keystone, which bears a Maltese cross and the date 1647, is a reminder that Governor Montmagny, Champlain's successor, was a knight of the Order of Malta. We are indebted to this governor for the first urban map of the city. Some citizens of Québec took pity on this knight who had no mount and decided to get him a horse. This is how the first horse arrived in New France in the summer of 1647.

The Château Frontenac takes its name from Louis Buade, Count Frontenac, Governor of New France at the end of the seventeenth century.

Governor Frontenac played an important role in New France. Along with Talon, the first Intendant, Frontenac contributed to the reorganization of the colony. He had rather an unusual personality, though, and often fell out with the people around him; the latter included Monseigneur de Laval, the governor of Montréal, and his own wife, who never accompanied him to New France. At the end of his life, Frontenac, in a moment of sentimentality, requested that his body be buried in the chapel of the Récollets but that his heart be sent to his wife, Anne de la Grange. On his death the governor's strange request was carried out. The silver box containing the heart of her impetuous husband was carried to the Countess. Anne, the "divine", refused the casket and sent it back to New France declaring that she could not be united in death to him from whom she had been separated all her life. When the small casket was returned to New France, the chapel of the Récollets had recently burned down so Frontenac's remains were buried in the Québec Cathedral.

A great many dignitaries have stayed at the Château Frontenac: Charles Lindbergh, several members of the royal family including Queen Elizabeth II, Charles de Gaulle, Alfred Hitchcock, Anne Baxter, Montgomery Clift, Jackie Gleason, Grace of Monaco, Jack Dempsey, and Bing Crosby. Two provincial premiers, Maurice Duplessis and Daniel Johnson, had accommodations in the Château Frontenac during their mandates.

Many important events have taken place in the Château Frontenac. When in August 1943 and September 1944, the

Sir Winston Churchill

Allied leaders met in Québec to discuss the conducting of the war and future strategy, the different delegations were accommodated at the Château. For security reasons, only Prime Minister Churchill and President Roosevelt were housed at the Québec Citadel. All of the others, including Lord Mountbatten and Mr. Anthony Eden, stayed at the Château. There were more than 500 Allied personnel and the daily cost was more than 8 000 dollars. It is reported that Lord Mountbatten profited from his stay in Québec to see the steep cliff which the English forces led by Wolfe climbed to reach the heights of Québec on September 13, 1759.

At the time of the first conference, the Normandy landing and the attack on Japan were discussed. If it had not been for the loyalty of Sergeant Emile Couture, the adopted strategy could have been discovered. Sergeant Couture was in charge of the material organization of the conference. He had been asked to move several desks and, while doing so, he discovered a note book in which were mentioned the date of the Normandy landing (between the 6th and the 8th of June 1944, depending on weather conditions), the names of the men in charge (General Montgomery and Lord Mountbatten), the points of attack, the number of soldiers and also a plan X to crush Japan. Sergeant Couture informed his superiors of his discovery, although not without some difficulty. He kept the secret until the end of the war and his loyalty earned him the medal of the Empire.

The Wolfe-Montcalm Monument

The Gazette de Québec announced, in August 1827, that Lord Dalhousie, the Governor of Canada, wished to have a monument erected to the memory of Generals Montcalm and Wolfe who had died on the battlefield on September 13, 1759. The sketch designed by Captain Young was accepted and on November 15, 1827, Governor Dalhousie presided over the laying of the first stone. The monument was inaugurated on September 8, 1828, the very day of Lord Dalhousie's departure for England.

The obelisk bears two Latin inscriptions attributed to John Charlton Fisher, director of the Gazette. They can be translated as follows:

1. "Their courage gave them a common death,
History a common fame.
Posterity a common monument.

2. The foundation stone of this monument, erected to the memory of two famous men, Wolfe and Montcalm,

neglected for many years, was laid by George, Earl of Dalhousie, Governor of the English possessions in North America. A work worthy of a distinguised leader, this monument was raised up by his power, stimulated by his example, favoured by his generosity, under the reign of George IV of England in the year of grace 1827."

The American Consulate

A few steps west of the Wolfe-Montcalm monument, on the corner of Sainte-Geneviève and Dufferin Terrace, is the American Consulate. This building was restored in the early 1950's. It recalls the important American contribution to the history of the city. Beyond the battles and the economic and political relations, the events linking the two communities are numerous.

The fourth part of this guidebook entitled "Québec City and the North American Continent" summarizes the main features of this relationship. For instance, we will learn that the daughter of one of the prisoners taken by the French

William Lyon Mackenzie King,
F.D. Roosevelt,
Sir Winston Churchill and
Earl Athlone.
(Archives de la ville de Québec – Canada – National Film Board)

during the raid on Deerfield, Massachusetts, in 1704, was the ancestor of Monseigneur Plessis, the eleventh Bishop of Québec.

From the Jardin des Gouverneurs to Place D'Armes

From the Jardin des Gouverneurs, you can, by passing under the main archway of the Château Frontenac, return to the Place d'Armes or go up rue Mont-Carmel to the park of the same name. There you can take advantage of the serenity of the spot. Notice Maison Bédard, 18 Mont-Carmel, and Maison Feldman, with its Anglo-Norman style, built around 1832, at 24 Mont-Carmel. Maison Bédard owes its name to Pierre Bédard, founder of the newspaper Le Canadien, and to his son, Elzéar, mayor of Québec in 1833-1834. A plaque on No 31 recalls that at the end of the seventeenth century a "cavalier", a defensive work situated behind the main fortifications, was erected on the heights of Mont-Carmel. From parc Mont-Carmel, walk back toward the Château Frontenac and go through the main archway to Place d'Armes. The first part of your visit to the city ends here.

The Taschereau Monument

FOOTLOOSE IN QUÉBEC: Second part

From Place d'Armes, you take du Trésor and Buade to the Taschereau monument in the place de la Basilique. Rue or ruelle, du Trésor (of the treasure or revenue), was so named because it once led to the offices of the treasurer of the naval troops. As for rue Buade, it recalls the reign of Louis de Buade, comte de Palluau et de Frontenac, Governor of New France from 1672 to 1682 and from 1689 to 1698.

1. THE TASCHEREAU MONUMENT OR THE CATHOLIC PRESENCE IN QUÉBEC

Monseigneur E.-A. Taschereau

The statue of Cardinal Taschereau, in bronze the colour of old-gold, was cast in the workshops of Berbedienne of Paris, under the direction of A. Vermare. Its pedestal is made of red granite from New Brunswick and the terrace of blue granite from Rivière-à-Pierre, Québec. The bas relief recalls three important moments in the Cardinals's life: the institution of the Quarante-Heures (Forty Hours) in 1872; his ministering to the typhoid victims during their quarantine on Grosse-Ile in 1847; and his role as superior of the Séminaire de Québec and as rector of Université Laval, of which he was one of the founders.

Elzéar-Alexandre Taschereau was born on February 17, 1820, in Sainte-Marie, Beauce county. He was the first Canadian cardinal. In fact, the subsequent cardinals would all be chosen from the archdiocese of Québec up until 1953, a fact which illustrates the historical importance and the role Québec played as Mother church and primatial seat of Canadian Catholicism. The tradition was broken in 1953 when the cardinalship passed to Monseigneur Paul-Émile Léger, Bishop of Montréal (and not to Monseigneur Maurice Roy of the Québec diocese). Apparently, some Québécois consoled themselves at the time with a pun on the two names, stating that it was better to have a bishop "roi" (king) than a cardinal "léger" (light, slight).

Some historians claim that political reasons dictated the choice of the first Canadian cardinal in 1886. At the end of the last century, after the hanging of Louis Riel, a patriot who fought for the cause of the Métis and the Francophones of Western Canada, Canada was sharply divided into two factions: the first, made up primarily of Anglophones, approved the decision of the federal government not to commute Riel's death sentence; while the other faction, primarily composed of Francophones, opposed it. The event led to a renewal of Québec nationalism and favoured the election of Québec Premier Honoré Mercier, whose national views left no doubt. In an attempt to calm Québec agitation and create a climate of diversion, some "Canadians" counted on the religious sentiments of the "Québécois" and exerted their influence on London and Westminster to have Rome name the Archibishop of Québec to the cardinalship. At the time, there was some rivalry between the religious authorities of Québec and Montréal, centered primarily around the foundation of the Catholic universities. In order not to fuel the fire, Rome elevated the diocese of Montréal to an archdiocese.

The Establishment of Christianity in New France

At the time of the great discoveries, the Papacy still played an important political role. In 1493, Rome had divided the new lands between Spain and Portugal by the Treaty of Tordesillas. In order to remain in the good graces of the Vatican, France added a Christian dimension to its colonial policy. But its first ordinances were of a general nature. Prostestants and Catholics shared the command of the first missions in America. Discrimination against Protestants did not begin until the seventeenth century.

The second article of the charter of the Compagnie des Cent-Associés, founded in 1627, specified that the colonists to New France had to be of the Catholic faith. The repeal of the Edict of Nantes in 1685 legalized discrimination against Protestants. From this time on, with a few exceptions, the inhabitants of New France would be Catholic.

The Récollets

The Récollet Fathers were the first members of a religious order to settle in Québec. Shortly after their arrival in 1615, they erected a small chapel, a few steps from Champlain's Habitation, where the first religious acts performed in Québec took place — the first mass, the first marriages... The building was later destroyed. In 1620, the Récollets built their first monastery on the banks of the Rivière Saint-Charles. In 1692, they abandoned this site leaving it to the Hôpital Général de Québec and built a new monastery in the Upper Town, on the spot where the Anglican Cathedral would be built after the destruction of the Récollet monastery at the end of the eighteenth century.

The Récollets, like the Jesuits, were obliged to leave the colony during the English occupation of 1629 to 1632. They finally returned to New France in 1670 at the request of Intendant Talon, who wanted a counter-weight to the influence of the Bishop and the Jesuits. The Récollets, priests in charge, missionaries, almoners and military, were, on the whole, fairly close to the civil and military administrations. During the dispute between Talon and Monseigneur de Laval regarding brandy, they were on the side of the Intendant.

Shortly after the Conquest, the Récollets were no longer allowed to recruit new members. The community disappeared with the passing of the last Récollet father, Arthur Louis dit Bonami, to whom we owe the rescuing of the flag of Carillon during the fire which ravaged the Récollet monastery in 1796.

The Jesuits

The Jesuits were the first members of a religious order to come to New France. They settled Acadia as early as 1611. They reached Québec in 1625. They first stayed with the Récollets and then built a residence in 1626 at the confluence of the rivières Lairet and Saint-Charles, where Jacques Cartier and his companions wintered in 1535-1536. In 1635, the Jesuits founded their college, the first in North America. There they gave courses on hydrography subsidized by the king. This college was destroyed by fire in 1640, rebuilt in 1642 and enlarged in 1725. After the Conquest, the Jesuits, like the other communities, were no longer allowed to receive novices. The college served then as a barracks for English soldiers. It was demolished in 1877 to make way for the present Hôtel de ville (City Hall).

At the end of the last century, the old City Hall, situated at 76 Saint-Louis, no longer met the needs of the municipality. In 1889, the city acquired the former land of the Jesuits for some 20 000 dollars and undertook the construction of the present building, at a cost of 144 484 dollars. It was officially inaugurated on September 15, 1896.

In 1637, benefiting from a gift from Noël Brûlart, seigneur of Sillery, the Jesuits established a mission a few kilometres west of Québec. They built a residence which, destroyed by fire in 1657, was immediately rebuilt. This building, probably the oldest house in Canada, was recently restored and opened to the public.

The work of the Jesuits is considerable. They were priests in charge in the parishes of Notre-Dame de Québec until

1664, of Ville-Marie (Montreal) until 1657 and of Trois-Rivières until 1760. The Jesuit Fathers were primarily known for their work as missionaries.

Often at the risk of their lives, they never hesitated to carry the "good news" to the heart of the Iroquois territory where they came into conflict with the chaman, the Amerindian witch doctor. They stood for a civilization which was completely foreign to the autochthons who often set up a strong resistance. The Jesuit Relations recall, in speaking of the Jesuit martyr Father Gabriel Lallement, that Father Lallement "raised his eyes to heaven, clasped his hands together from time to time, and sighed, invoking God's help. He had been struck by a hatchet on the left ear. The blow went so deep that the brain was exposed. We could see no part of his body, from his feet to his head, which had not been scorched and where he was not burned raw, even his eyes, where these ungodly beings had stuck live coals."[1]

The Jesuits were also explorers. Father Alvanel went as far as Hudson's Bay; Father Marquette and Louis Jolliet, a former student of the Jesuits, discovered the Mississippi; and Father DeQuen, Lac Saint-Jean. They also occupied very important administrative posts. Having been endowed with considerable goods, they were bestowed the grand curacy of Louisiana and that of Michillimakinac. If they were joined together as a single piece of land, the Jesuit holdings would have covered an area about 10 kilometres wide and 300 kilometres deep. They brought in annually to their owners some 20 000 pounds, in addition to the 13 300 pounds accorded to their Québec college for the upkeep of their missions and their chair of hydrography.

The Séminaire de Québec

The Séminaire de Québec was founded in 1663 by Monseigneur de Laval and was first set up in a house bought from the widow of Guilllaume Couillard. The construction of its buildings began with the wing of parlors in 1675. The plans were drawn up by Frère Luc, a Récollet. The wing of the Sainte-Famille (Holy Family), today "la Procure" (the office of the procurator), was built between the years 1678 and 1681; and the interior chapel, in 1694. The first buildings were destroyed by two different fires, in 1701 and 1705, but they were quickly rebuilt. It underwent certain transformations in 1822, and five years later a new wing was added to the 1681 building. The present chapel was constructed after the original chapel burned down in 1888. In spite of the many fires (1701, 1705, 1865 and 1888), the

Séminaire remains today an excellent example of seventeenth-century architecture. The original basements of the 1678 building, as well as the vaulted kitchens, can still be seen. The Séminaire has preserved many valuable articles which are today part of our national heritage. It was here in the Séminaire de Québec that the American officers, captured during the attack on Québec in 1775 and 1776, were held prisoner.

During the French Régime, the life of the seminarist was quite austere. The young man had to spend the whole of the school year in the Séminaire. After August 15, the start of the annual vacation, he went to the farm at Saint-Joachim (owned by the institution) to work in the fields. Once the holidays were over, the student returned to the Séminaire, which was at that time a training school. The students lived at the Séminaire but took their courses at the Collège des Jésuites. When this college closed shortly after the Conquest, the seminary began to offer courses. Of the 843 students enrolled in the Petit Séminaire de Québec during the French Régime, 118 became priests.

The old wing of the Séminaire (1678) with its sundial (1773)

The Arrival of the First Nuns

The year 1639 marks the arrival of the first two female communities in New France; the Ursulines and the Hospitalières de la Miséricorde de Jésus (the Hospitallers of the Mercy of Jesus). The Ursulines, guided by the venerable Mother Marie de l'Incarnation devoted themselves to the training of French and Amerindian girls. They first occupied a building in Place Royale but later moved to the Upper Town. On November 21, 1642, they moved into the convent which they have occupied to the present day. As for the Hospitalières, they were entrusted with the running of the Hôtel-Dieu Hospital.

In 1693, at the request of Monseigneur de Saint-Vallier, the Hospitalières replaced the Sisters of the Congregation of Notre-Dame in the running of the Hôpital Général de Québec. The Sisters of the Congregation, a community founded in Montréal in 1658 by Marguerite Bourgeois, remained in Québec and continued to take care of a convent established in 1692 in Québec's Lower Town, at the corner of Saint-Pierre and Côte de la Montagne (Mountain Hill); and of their mission on the Ile d'Orléans. In 1843, they moved to a new convent in the Saint-Roch district.

A Triumphant Church

In the course of the nineteenth century, and more particularly after 1850, a number of religious communities came to swell the ranks of the pioneer communities. From the second half of the century on, the Catholic Church became a progressively more important force in the heart of the French-speaking community where it exerted a very influential leadership.

Many different elements helped to elevate the church to a place of prominence — the political realignment which came about shortly after the Rebellion of 1837-1838, the failure of secularism, the sublimation of nationalism by a religious ideal and a certain rurality. "Between 1850 and 1901, the numbers of religious in communities increased from 243 to 1984, and the number of nuns in communities, from 650 to 6 628. To this number must be added the approximately 3 500 nuns who exercised their ministry outside of Québec in 1900."(2) Mother church, primatial seat of Catholicism in Canada, the only diocese in the province until 1830, holder of the cardinalship until 1953, the church of Québec knew how to profit from the increase in religious fervour and how to exert its leadership. Université Laval, founded in Québec in 1852, would remain the only Catholic and French-speaking university in the province for nearly seventy years. Around 1920, the city of Montréal, the metropolis of Canada and the largest French-speaking city in America, finally obtained a Catholic and French university, independant of Université Laval.

The Basilique (Basilica)

The first parish church of Québec was built at the request of Champlain. The founder of Québec had promised to erect a church to the Virgin Mary if New France, occupied by the English in 1627, was restored to France. When this happened in 1632, Champlain kept his promise and, the following year, the Church of Notre Dame de la Recouvrance (Our Lady of Recovery) was built south of the present-day Basilique. The spot is commemorated by a plaque, an initiative of the Québec Historical Society, at 15 Buade Street. A few feet from the church, at 9½ Buade, stood the Champlain Chapel, built in 1636, to the memory of the founder of Québec. A fire in 1640 destroyed the Notre-Dame de la Recouvrance Church and the Champlain Chapel, along with all of the early registers of the colony. Worshipers had to gather at the building of the Compagnie des Cent-Associés while waiting for the completion of their new church in 1650. In 1674, with the nomination of the first Québec bishop, it was raised to the rank of cathedral. As for the Champlain Chapel, it was rebuilt, but was later destroyed in 1660 by an earthquake. The cathedral was enlarged several times and restored in 1748; the plans for the restoration were drafted by Chaussegros de Lery. Eleven years later, during the Conquest, it was once again reduced to ruins. The faithful had to worship in the Ursuline and Séminaire chapels. A new church was built within the old walls. The woodwork, sculptures, and architecture of the new building, built between the years 1768 and 1771, were the work of the Baillairgé family. This cathedral, which had been raised to the rank of basilica at the end of the last century, again fell victim to fire on December 22, 1922. Reportedly, an American set fire to it in the hope of profiting from the ensuing confusion to rob the church. The basilica was rebuilt in 1925.

Collected within the Basilique are many treasures, especially old paintings, both originals and copies, and silverworks dating from the French Régime. In the crypts of the Basilique and the Séminaire lie the remains of more than 900 people including several bishops, five French governors, and the hero of the story of the "Chien d'or" (The

Golden Dog), Nicolas Jacquin dit Philibert. Here they "sleep their last sleep".

The Place du Marché (Market Square)

The square across from the Basilique was once bustling with life. It was the site of the Upper-Town market, Notre-Dame market. The first Québec market was that of Place Royale. Later the Lower Town had several other markets. The Finlay market was located across from Place Royale, The Champlain market, west of Place Royale near the former Cul-de-Sac Cove, was built in 1854 with the stone retrieved from the first Parliament building which had burned down some time earlier. The market itself was destroyed by fire in 1899. There was also the Jacques-Cartier market near du Roi and de la Couronne, and the Saint-Paul market on rue Saint-Paul. In the Upper Town, there was the Montcalm market, Place d'Youville, and the Notre-Dame market across from the Basilique. Here a circular hall was built (as shown in the Duberger model) but later demolished.

Côte de la Fabrique (Manufacturers Hill)

The first tavern in Québec was opened near the Notre-Dame market at 22 Côte de la Fabrique. In 1648, the governor of New France recognized Jacques Boisdon as the first and only inn-keeper "on the condition that his house be emptied of unknown people and closed during religious offices". It is reported that the sacristan from the cathedral used to go there and pass his cane under each bed to make sure that no one was hiding there.

In 1783, new obligations fell upon the tavern-keepers of the city. According to a by-law, "each tavern-keeper, inn-keeper or café owner will have installed outside his door, by the first of next December, a lamp which will light the street, from dusk to midnight (except when the moon shines), under penalty of a five shilling fine for each night the owner neglects or refuses to conform to this article."

Cafés have always been popular in Québec but they were especially so during the days of the English garrison. But those who did not care for the atmosphere which reigned there or who lacked the means of frequenting cafés could always make their own liqueur. The recipe was quite simple:

1 lemon chopped fine	3 soup-spoons of molasses
1 pound of sugar	1 gallon of water

Stir the ingredients for ten minutes. Let the mixture set. Put a slice of bread soaked in barm to float on the top. Cover for 24 hours. Strain and bottle. Seal hermetically without having completely filled the bottle. Drink after eight days.

A plaque at 42 de la Fabrique recalls the bookstore of the Crémazie brothers. In the middle of the nineteenth century, their bookstore was the meeting-place of Quebec's intellectual élite. A poor administrator, Octave Crémazie was forced to evade his creditors by secretly fleeing to France in the autumn of 1862. On the occasion of the centenary celebrations of the French victory at Carillon, Octave Crémazie had composed a poem which earned him the title of "National poet".

From the Place de la Basilique (Basilica Square) to the Anglican Cathedral

From the monument Taschereau, you go up rue Desjardins to the Anglican Cathedral.

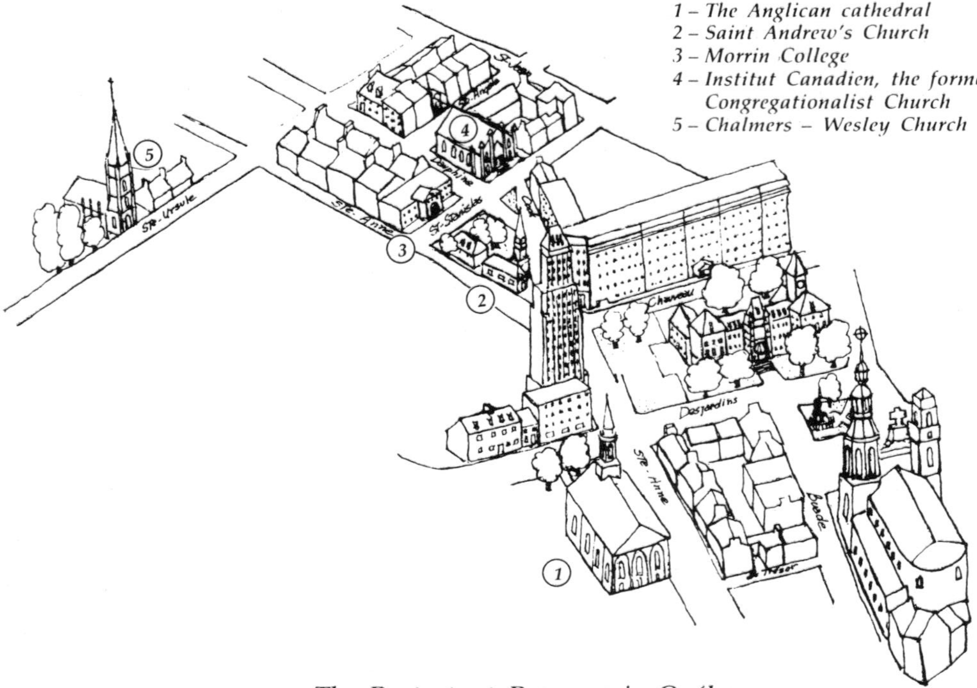

1 – The Anglican cathedral
2 – Saint Andrew's Church
3 – Morrin College
4 – Institut Canadien, the former Congregationalist Church
5 – Chalmers – Wesley Church

The Protestant Presence in Québec

2. THE ANGLICAN CATHEDRAL OR THE PROTESTANT PRESENCE IN QUÉBEC

The Cathedral

The Anglican Cathedral, Holy Trinity, was the first one to be built outside of the United Empire and is one of the oldest religious buildings in Québec. It was constructed in 1804, on the site where the Récollet monastery once stood.

Shortly after the Conquest of 1759, the Anglicans used the monastery chapel for divine service. When the building was destroyed by fire in 1796, the Anglicans had to use the chapel of the old Jesuit college, which had been transformed into a barracks. This building was already being used by Catholics and the Anglican Bishop did not like the joint use of a building which was, furthermore, not a suitable place of worship. He requested the building of a church for the exclusive use of Anglicans and the King granted his request in 1799. The first stone of the new building was laid on August 11, 1804.

Holy Trinity Cathedral is a fine exemple of the Palladian order of architecture. Built at the expense of the Crown and modelled after the church of Saint-Martin-in-the-Fields in London, it measures about 30 metres by 20 metres. The tower, 50 metres high, houses a carillon of eight bells, and was the first of its kind in Canada. There are, today, only six of these carillons and two of them are found in Québec City: one in the Holy Trinity Cathedral and the other in the old Anglican church on rue Saint-Jean, a gift of the Anglican community to the city. This old church is now used as a library. The pews in the Anglican Cathedral are made of oak; the wood comes from the royal forest at Windsor Castle, England. The royal pew, which is at the front of the left gallery and which is reserved for the Sovereign or his representative, is particularly remarkable. The Anglican Cathedral numbers among its many treasures an altar facing used during the coronation of George III in Westminster Abbey and a collection of silver-work. the Cathedral organ is of excellent craftmanship and is used during concerts which are greatly appreciated by music lovers. In the north-east corner of the Close, there once stood a large elm. Tradition has it that it was under the shade of this tree, cut down in 1845, that Champlain smoked the peace pipe with the Amerindians who first occupied the site. The Bishop's throne was made from the wood of this tree.

Immediately following the Conquest, the Anglican Church of Québec was responsible to the diocese of Nova

Scotia. The Diocese of Québec was created in 1793. The first Lord Bishop was Jacob Mountain. The Mountain family was to play an important role in the establishment of the Anglican faith in Canada. The uncle and the cousin of Quebec's first bishop became priests of the diocese and the latter's son, George, became, in 1837, the third Bishop of Québec.

During the time of the Mountains, the Québec diocese extended from New Brunswick west to Upper Canada (Ontario). The territory beyond Upper Canada was directly answerable to the authority of the Bishop of London. The Québec diocese was later subdivided; in 1839, the diocese of Toronto was created and, in 1850, the diocese of Montréal.

The Protestant Presence in the Province of Québec

The Protestant presence in the province of Québec dates back to the early days of the colony. Profiting from a certain religious freedom, the Protestants took part in the first expeditions to New France. Champlain's companion, De Monts, was of the Protestant faith. In 1541, Cartier, a Catholic, served under Roberval, a Protestant. François I had ordered the discoverer of Canada to instruct the Amerindians in the "love and fear of God and in His holy law and Christian doctrine". But this ordinance was of a general nature and no religion was singled out. By adding the evangelization of the autochthons to the objectives of colonization, the French authorities hoped merely to attract the favour of the Vatican. Furthermore, the first baptism in New France did not take place until 1610, seventy years after the voyages of Jacques Cartier.

The first ordinance in favour of Catholicism dates back to the year 1588. It was later applied to all other concessions and gradually Protestants were expelled from New France. In 1627, article II of the charter of the Compagnie des Cent-Associés ordered the associates to populate the colony with "French Catholic natives". The repeal of the Edict of Nantes in 1685 legalized religious discrimination in favour of Catholics. Henceforth, Protestantism was legally excluded from New France.

Outside of the edicts and ordinances, the Protestant presence was tolerated to a certain extent. Craftsmen were sought after and one had to accept them whatever their faith. Thus the founder of Montréal, Maisonneuve, whose Catholic fervour was beyond any doubt, accepted Protestant craftsmen at Ville-Marie. Other Protestants were to come as well — merchants, soldiers, prisoners of war, deserters of the American Thirteen Colonies, captives taken during

Québec vue de
l'Université Laval.
(Photo C. Gosselin)

Québec romantique.
(Photo M. Beaudoin)

raids, etc. During the French Régime, some 900 Protestants settled in New France, often under very difficult conditions.

In 1660, the city of Québec numbered only 600 inhabitants, of which about a hundred belonged to religious communities. The Protestants had to submit constantly to Catholic pressure, especially after the repeal of the Edict of Nantes. They had to register certificates in the Catholic cult: baptism, marriage, burial. They were forced to sign certificates of renunciation and were excluded from certain trades. For instance, they were not allowed to be apothecaries or midwives. Under such difficult conditions, many Protestants sought to pass unnoticed. They officially joined the Catholic faith, although they remained Protestants in their hearts.

Shortly after the Conquest, they were somewhat revenged. The compulsory swearing of the Oath (Serment du Test) to which no Catholic could submit without renouncing his faith, allowed Protestants access to public duties and government contracts to the detriment of Catholics.

The Protestants H.T. Cramahé, J. Bruyères and G. Maturien were named secretaries in the governments of Montréal, Trois-Rivières, and Québec. Louis de Mestral was named adjutant of the government of Trois-Rivières in 1762. Various tasks were confided to other French Protestants; Jean Martheilhe obtained the contract to repair the chapel of the Récollet monastery at Québec and François Lévesque became the depositary of the Forges du Saint-Maurice. As of 1774, the Serment du Test was no longer compulsory.

The numbers of the Protestant community increased considerably immediately after the Conquest. The arrival of a number of English regiments, the presence of the English garrison up until 1871, the economic role played by the city of Québec, and the fact that it was the capital of the Canadian colony attracted a great many immigrants who swelled the ranks of the English Protestant community. In the middle of the last century, 40 percent of the inhabitants of the city of Québec were English speaking. Many monuments and buildings testify to this very important presence.

Saint Andrew's Presbyterian Church was built in 1809 on rue Sainte-Anne. Its tower is a replica of that of the Anglican Cathedral. In 1862, thanks to a gift from one of its members, Doctor Joseph Morrin, the Presbyterian community undertook the restoration of the old provincial prison on rue Saint-Stanislas with the intention of turning it into a university, known under the name of Morrin College.

This old prison, built in 1810 and replaced around 1860 by the one in the Plains of Abraham, had, at one time, a

Rev. G. J. Mountain

famous "boarder" — Philippe Aubert de Gaspé, the author of the novel "les Anciens Canadiens" (Canadians of Old). He was imprisoned for the debt of 789 583 dollars, a rather considerable sum for the times. Thanks to a petition raised by his fellow citizens, De Gaspé was finally released, having been imprisoned for three years, four months, and five days. At the time of his imprisonment, the De Gaspé family lived on rue Sainte-Anne. It is reported that, during long sleepless nights, the prisoner watched from his cell the lights in his home which indicated that his children, often ill, were being attended to.

For many years, Morrin College housed the Québec Literary and Historical Society, the first Canadian literary society, founded by Lord Dalhousie, Governor of Canada, on January 6, 1824. The Society's library is still located in this building.

The Congregationalists built their first church on rue Ferland and another on rue McMahon. In 1848, they constructed on the corner of Sainte-Angèle and Dauphine streets, a building which is a replica of the church of Minard Lalever in the United States. It was later given to the city of Québec and now houses the Institut Canadien, a literary and humanist club founded in the middle of the last century, and a municipal library.

After the year 1820, the Holy Trinity Cathedral no longer met the needs of the Anglican community. Hence, Saint Matthew's Church was constructed in 1822 on rue Saint-Jean. Trinity Chapel was built some two years later on Saint-Stanislas, and Saint Michael's Church, in 1854, in the suburb of Sillery. Some years later, a chapel was erected at Limoilou. Today, Trinity Chapel is used by the Conservatoire d'art dramatique (The Conservatory of Dramatic Art) of Québec. Saint Matthew's Church was given to the city of Québec and converted into a municipal library.

In the middle of the last century, former Congregationalists joined the ranks of the Presbyterian Church of Canada, founded in 1844, and erected their first building on rue Saint-Ursule, Chalmers' Church. George Brown, an important political figure, was one of the pioneers of this church. The head of the Clear Grit party of Canada West, he suggested, in 1864, a coalition government in the elaboration of the project for Canadian confederation. A fierce adversary of Catholicism, he campaigned against the creation of separate schools (Catholic) in Upper Canada and he played a role in the incident known as the "Gavazzi riot".

At one time a fervent Catholic, Alessandro Gavazzi became disillusioned with the national policy of Pius IX. He left Italy for England where he began to fight the church of his childhood. Invited by a Protestant association to come to America, Gavazzi, with the encouragement and support of George Brown, gave many lectures in Canada. His passage through Montréal occasioned a riot which left seven people dead and a great many injured. In Québec City on June 6, 1853, the Irish Catholics went to Chalmers' Church to hear this virulent preacher. Angered by his comments, they stormed the pulpit and knocked down the visitor who narrowly escaped death. Gavazzi finally returned to Montréal under police escort.

In 1931, the Methodists of the Wesleyan Church joined the members of the Presbyterian Church. Both congregations belonged to the United Church of Canada and the church took the name of Chalmers Wesley United Church.

Many buildings are witness to the important Protestant presence in the City of Québec during the last century. A house, on the corner of des Glacis and Saint-Oliver streets, now owned by the Soeurs de la Charité (The Sisters of Charity), was the site of the first Jeffery Hale's Hospital. A building in Place d'Youville recalls the founding of the Y.M.C.A. in Québec. Many other buildings, such as Saint John's Chapel and the Finlay Asylum, have been destroyed.

The Protestant presence and, to a great extent, the Anglophone presence in the city of Québec is less considerable now than it was during the last century. In 1850, it represented almost half of the population of the city, about 10 percent in 1900, and makes up less than 5 percent at the present time.

The departure of the English-speaking Protestant community from Québec City was due greatly to the shifting of economic activity towards central Canada. This economic displacement can be explained by the decline of maritime activity in the second half of the nineteenth century, the end of the shipbuilding era, the departure of the English garrison in 1871, the choice of Ottawa as the new Canadian capital, and by the restructuring of the Canadian economy.

From the Anglican Cathedral to rue Saint-Jean

From the Anglican Cathedral, you take rue Sainte-Anne in the direction of rue Cook. The Hotel Clarendon, on the corner of Sainte-Anne and Desjardins, was built in 1858, from the plans drafted by Charles Baillargé. "This building", according to the Journal de Québec of December 24, 1868, "is laid out in such a way that it can be converted into

four first class residences. It is four storeys high, in red brick, with a ground-floor in freestone. The height of its walls from the ground is 60 feet (20 metres) by 85 feet (26 metres) wide and 45 feet (15 metres) deep." The neighbouring building, the Price Building, was built in 1930. This edifice, a fine example of Art Deco, was for a long time, the tallest building in the city. Notice on the corner of Sainte-Anne and Cook streets, Saint Andrew's Church. From the Presbyterian church, go along Cook and Dauphine to rue Saint-Stanislas. On your left, you have Morrin College, and, on your right, the Institut Canadien, a former Methodist church. Continue along Dauphine to Saint-Ursule in the direction of Saint-Jean. From the corner of Dauphine and Sainte-Ursule, you can see, beyond the first houses, the steeple of Chalmers Wesley United Church.

The Duchess d'Aiguillon

1 – Porte Saint-Jean
2 – Hôtel-Dieu de Québec
3 – Maison Montcalm

Rue Saint-Jean

3. RUE SAINT-JEAN, THE START OF THE KING'S ROAD

A Short History

Rue Saint-Jean starts at the corners of la Fabrique, Garneau, and Couillard streets, and extends as far as chemin Sainte-Foy to the west. It was named after Jean Bourdon who settled a few arpents to the west of the colony on côte Ste-Geneviève in 1640. Jean Bourdon laid out a path leading to his residence. This later became rue Saint-Jean.

The street became a commercial thoroughfare very early on. Around 1800, Joseph Bouchette, Surveyor-General of Lower Canada, wrote, "Saint-Jean, de Buade, de la Fabrique and most of Côte du Palais can be considered the business section of the Upper Town. We find wholesale and retail merchants and a large number of innkeepers; as a result, these streets are certainly the busiest of all of them".(4)

General Murray, Wolfe's brigadier during the Siege of Québec in 1759, Commander-in-Chief of the British Army of Canada, Governor of Québec and of Canada from 1760 to 1768, acquired a house on rue Saint-Jean on March 9, 1764. Rebuilt around 1824, this property situated at 1078 Saint-Jean was classified an historic monument on September 25, 1963. It is now known as the maison Murray-Adams. A man named Adams was its owner at the time of its naming.

After the Conquest, General Murray knew that he could not govern without taking into account the large Francophone majority. He favoured the nomination of the first Catholic bishop after the Conquest. Considering the French Canadians as his most loyal subjects, he felt the wrath of the Anglophone merchants whom he described as a "clique of merchants who rushed to a country where there is no money, who believe they are superior in station and wealth to the soldiers and the Canadians, and who like to consider the former as merceneries and the latter as slaves from birth".(5)

In 1766, Murray had to return to England to defend his policies. He won his case and remained the governor of Canada until 1768.

A plaque on the building at 1195 Saint-Jean is a reminder of the brilliant career of the jeweller Cyrille Duquet, pioneer in the bringing of the telephone to Québec. In 1877, he installed the first telephone line which connected his shop in the Upper Town to his other store in the Lower Town. The following year, he obtained a patent for his "French

telephone", an instrument which contained both a microphone and a listening device which is now used the world over. It is believed that the same year Duquet succeeded in using telephone lines between Montréal and Québec those used by Bell had a working radius of only a dozen or so miles. In 1882, he sold his rights to the Bell Telephone Company of Canada. We are also in his debt for the invention of a time clock which was sold to the New Haven Clock Company.

Now, rue Saint-Jean is still business oriented, but other activities have been added. The presence of numerous boutiques, restaurants, bars, and discothèques make it one of the most popular spots on the "Quebec by night" circuit. During the Québec City Summer Festival, for example, the street is often closed to traffic. People meet there late at night, much to the discontent of the residents of the area who would like to go back to the old days when they could "walk down rue Saint-Jean" in peace and quiet.

The house located at the corner of Saint-Jean and Côte du Palais is a reminder of another event — when the statue of St. John the Baptist was replaced by that of General Wolfe. The first owner of the house had placed, in a niche outside the front of his home, a statue of St. John the Baptist. After the Conquest, the owner, who was afraid of offending the victors, thought it best to remove the statue, which, according to Philippe Aubert de Gaspé, was relocated at the Hôtel Dieu Hospital.

Several years later, butcher George Hipps, acquired the property and decided to redecorate the empty niche. It was decided that a statue of General Wolfe would be erected and it quickly became part of the surroundings — hence the name "Wolfe's Corner". At the end of the 1830's, the statue disappeared. At that time, relations between Francophones and Anglophones were particularly strained, and it was immediately thought that the misdeed was the work of the patriots. This explanation, although plausible, was not the case.

Returning one night from the old Hotel Albion, on Côte de la Fabrique, some sailors from the "Inconstant" which was anchored in the port of Québec, noticed the General, and, deciding that he looked unhappy, elected to take him with them to Bermuda. "Maybe," they said, "the sun will give him back some of his gaiety". Thus the General left for Bermuda and did not return to Québec City until several years later... To his great surprise, the mayor of

Québec City found, in a package addressed to him, the statue of the General, which he quickly restored to its niche.

By 1898, the weather had done its work. The statue was rapidly deteriorating. It was moved to the library of the Literary and Historical Society situated at Morrin College on rue Saint-Stanislas. Another statue was raised in the niche of the butcher Hipps's house where it remained until quite recently.

The Porte Saint-Jean

The first porte Saint Jean was built in 1693, according to plans by engineer Boisberthelot de Beaucours. It formed part of the first fortifications situated to the east near rue Sainte-Ursule. It was moved to its present site in 1720, and rebuilt according to plans by Chaussegros de Lery, Jr, in 1757, it was later repaired a number of times after by the English authorities. Once again demolished, it was reconstructed in 1867, only to be destroyed again in 1898. The present gate dates from 1939.

The "Chemin du Roy" (King's Road)

The "Chemin du Roy", the first direct road between Québec and Montréal, was inaugurated on August 5, 1734, when Lanouiller de Boisclerc, chief road-inspector for New France, left Québec by coach for Montréal. A plaque hung on porte Saint-Jean recalls this momentous occasion.

The construction of the "Kings'" Road marks an important stage in the development of road systems in New France. Hector Fabre recalls in his chronicles that it was a major affair, "an event in one's life to travel from Montréal to Québec City". The individual thought long about it and, before leaving, added a codicil to his will. His tearful family accompanied the hardy traveller to the port, giving last minute advice and saying emotional goodbyes. They jumped in the water to shake his hands one last time...

Sometimes, after a week of crosswinds, and sailing as much backward as foreward, he could still see the roof of his father's home and a waving kerchief saying goodbye like an untiring hand...

The trip sometimes lasted two weeks..."[6]

The construction of the chemin du Roy, started in 1706, took more than thirty years to complete. The inauguration took place in 1734. Masterpiece of road-inspectors Pierre

Robineau de Bécancour and Jean Eustache Lanouiller de Boisclerc, the King's Road, which was about three hundred kilometres long and 7,3 metres wide, greatly facilitated communications between the two biggest settlements in the colony. Even as recently as in 1840, a winter trip between Montréal and Québec City was "no small undertaking". The trip lasted two or two and a half days, depending on the condition of the road. The winter run between Montréal and Québec City was made by "mail" coaches, stage-coaches and "extra" vehicles. In the mail coaches there were seats for six to eight passengers. The state-coaches held the same number. Only the wealthy travelled by the "extra".

The "extra" was a sleigh drawn by two tandem driven horses. In the "extra", the relays were less frequent and the trip did not last as long as in the stage-coaches. Those who paid for the luxury of an "extra" were highly esteemed in the inns along the way. Ordinarily, these were deputies, judges, or wealthy industrialists. They had the right to drive in the middle of the road and the driver would call to the farmer with his horse and buggy "make way for the extra".

The rate for the extra was, one crown per league for two passengers. Only one passenger, travelling alone in a cart drawn by a single horse, paid thirty-six "sous" per league. Travellers by stage-coach paid 10$ for the passage between Montréal and Québec City, lodging and meals extra.

The vehicles travelled in five hour relays. The first stop on the return trip was the Deschamps inn, at the end of the Island (of Montréal) and the others were at Saint-Sulpice, Berthier, Rivière-du-Loup, (Louiseville), Trois-Rivières, Champlain, Sainte-Anne-de-la-Pérade, Deschambault, Pointe-aux-Trembles, (Neuville), and Québec City."[7]

The coming of the railway, in the second half of the 19th century, brought an end to the old fashioned stage-coaches and noticeably facilitated communication between the two cities but could not put an end to the mutual rivalry.

The Québec — Montréal Rivalry

Rivalry between the cities of Québec and Montréal dates back to the Amerindian period. In 1535, when Jacques Cartier, looking for a route to the west, decided to sail up the Saint-Laurent to Hochelaga (Montreal), the Amerindians of Stadacona (Quebec City) advised him against it. "Three Indians dressed up as devils — covered with dog skins, their faces painted black and wearing, of course, large horns, pretended to come from Hochelaga, where their god had predicted the death of the whites, under an excess of snow, ice and cold, if they ventured into that land."[8] The Amerindians of Stadacona wanted to keep for themselves the business monopoly which was going to be established in the St. Lawrence Valley and avoid being dominated by Hochelaga.

In 1642, the residents of Québec were opposed to the founding of Montréal. The population of the French colony at the time was very small and, fearing that the founding of Ville-Marie (Montréal) would imperil their own settlement, the citizens asked the founder of Ville-Marie to settle on the Île d'Orléans, which was nearer Québec City and easier to defend.

Maisonneuve was inflexible. He answered the residents of Québec, "and you will find I was right to start a colony there, even if all the trees on this island (Montréal) turn into as many Iroquois".

The rivalry between the two cities was to continue throughout the French Régime. The Montrealer Jeanne Mance tried to persuade Mme de la Peltrie, benefactress of the Ursuline Sisters of Québec City, to settle in Montréal.

Jean de Lauzon, Governor of New France, tried to detain immigrants including Marguerite Bourgeoys, who had been recruted by Maisonneuve, in Québec City. In the 1650's the establishment of the first bishopric in New France divided the clergy. The Sulpician fathers who had settled in Montréal, favoured of one of their own as bishop and the Jesuits of Québec City supported Mgr. Laval. The latter was chosen.

Frontenac, governor of the colony, tried to monopolize the fur trade to the detriment of Perrot, governor of the island of Montréal.

To the political, religious and economic conflicts were added quarrels over priority of importance between the bishop of Québec and the governor of Montréal, and between the governor of New France whose principal residence was located in Québec and the governor of Montréal. The squabbles over precedence were so numerous that it was necessary to draw up legislation regulating the question in 1716.

The economic stucture of the two cities was different. At that time, Montréal was a commercial centre dealing with the fur trade, while Québec was an administrative centre. The political, religious and military authorities set themselves up in Québec.

There was even, according to Pehr Kalm, a difference between the women of Montréal and the women of Québec. "There is, in Québec," he wrote in his diary of 1749, "a way of life which is too free, especially among married women whom, it seems, are introduced to numerous young Frenchmen that the Royal Navy brings over every year... These young officers, on the other hand, rarely come to Montréal. It can also be said, with certainty and without undermining the truth, that the women of Montréal and particularly young women are more diligent than their counterparts in Québec with respect to everything concerning housework."[9]

The city of Québec, well-situated at the narrowing of the fleuve Saint-Laurent, political and religious capital of New France and the Gilbraltar of America, had a certain authority over its rival, the city of Montréal, for as long as these advantages prevailed. Starting in the second half of the 19th century, Québec no longer held such a favourable position. The canalization of the Saint-Laurent, the invention of steam power, the development of the railways, and the smoothing out of Canadian-American relations, which eliminated the threat of war, led to the departure of the English garrison and the choice of Ottawa as the future capital of Canada. From the end of the 19th century on, Montréal became the new Canadian metropolis, leaving its rival only regional authority and some religious leadership which it did not delay in salvaging.

In the 1930's, it was thought that the old rivalry between the two cities had finally died. New circumstances, including the more active role of the provincial governments following the "Crash" of 1929, the development of provincial public works, the building up of the civil service sector, increased tourism, and the leadership exercised by the local Chamber of Commerce and by the Faculty of Social Sciences at Université Laval explain the partial economic recovery of the city. The old rivalry which people thought was dead and buried, re-emerged.

The citizens of Montréal attempted to take over projects started by the people of Québec. Montréal wanted to have a Winter Carnival but it was a failure. In Québec residents hurried to make the official burial during the 1962 Carnival ceremonies. On March 6, 1962, after a short ceremony, a coffin which symbolically represented the Montréal Carnival was thrown into the icy waters of the St. Lawrence, and then, It was no more... "For a long time the audience scrutinized the waves, for fear of seeing the symbolic sarcophagus reappear, containing the mortal remains of a "rascal" who had wanted to become more important than the one who had given it birth: The Québec Carnival."[10]

They also fought over the exclusivity of certain projects, such as the dispute over the creation of an international book show. Montréal also tried to stall or prevent certain activities from being carried out which would harm their market or reduce their sphere of influence. The difficult rise of the Québec "Nordiques" in the National Hockey League, is explained as follows. The Montréal Canadiens hesitated for a long time before accepting the sharing of television rights, fans and the beer market, (two breweries were directly involved in the conflict...)

The rivalry between Québec City and Montréal is not seen in the same light by Montrealers as by the people of Québec City. The importance of Montréal, the city's economic role and competition with Toronto no doubt explain the different levels of intensity... but no matter what people say, Montréal and Québec City will always be linked by the chemin du Roy.

From Rue Saint-Jean to the Hôtel-Dieu de Québec

From rue Sainte-Ursule, you now descend rue Saint-Jean to rue Collin and, from there, to rue Charlevoix where the Hôtel-Dieu Hospital is situated.

The Founding of the Hôtel-Dieu (Hospital) de Québec

The Hôtel-Dieu Hospital was the first hospital to be founded in North America. On August 16, 1637, an agreement was signed by the Duchess of Aiguillon, Cardinal Richelieu's niece, and the Hospitallières of the Hôtel-Dieu in Dieppe in order to establish a hospital in Québec. The Duchess of Aiguillon and Cardinal Richelieu guaranteed the funds necessary for its founding and the nuns offered their services.

Eighteen months later, on August 1st, 1639, the nuns finally arrived in Québec. Their arrival coincided with that of the Ursulines, who were dedicated to teaching. The fort's cannon heralded the event. The governor, the Knight of Montmagny, greeted the nuns on behalf of the inhabitants.

The Hospitalières, after having been temporarily lodged in the Upper Town in a house belonging to the Compagnie

des Cent-Associés, settled in Sillery, near the Jesuit monastery, which was built in 1637. The insecurity of the spot and the great distance which separated them from the city forced them to reconsider their choice. In 1644, the sisters returned to Québec City and built their hospital there. The official blessing of the new institution, by Father Barthélemy Vimont, took place on March 16, 1646.

Through the Years

The building has undergone numerous transformations since it was founded. In 1654, a main building and a church were added.

In 1665, Intendant Talon had a new building and a double patients' room built. The hospital was fitted with an aqueduct system. In 1755, two disgruntled sailors, it is said, set fire to the establishment, and it was completely destroyed. One nun died in the fire, but all of the patients were saved.

Two years later, a new building was inaugurated. After the Conquest, the hospital was requisitioned to billet English troops. The institution was not returned to its true vocation until 1784. The following year, thanks to the generosity of citizens and to compensation received from the occupying forces, two rooms were opened. In 1800, the present church was built. In 1816, the Hospital was again enlarged.

Other buildings followed in 1892, in 1925, and in 1930. In 1954, a fifteen-floor pavillion replaced the wings built in 1892 and in 1925 which, because of their "Renaissance" style, had blended much better with the architecture of the city than the present building.

Because of its geographical setting, the Hôtel-Dieu of Québec was one of the sites most exposed to assaults during the siege. In 1620, they say that in one attack, up to twenty-six cannonballs were collected within the walls of the cloister. The nuns rushed to deliver them to the French batteries so that they could be returned to the enemy. In 1775, during the American attack, the few nuns who did not flee to the Hôpital Général owed their lives to the sturdiness of the institution's vaults.

Robert Giffard, son-in-law of Louis Hébert, the first settler in New France, was the first doctor at the Hôtel-Dieu Hospital. His daughter, Françoise Giffard, was the first Canadian hospitalière. The first surgery at the Hôtel-Dieu Hospital was performed by Doctor Michel Sarrazin, on May 29, 1700. A nun from Montréal, Sister Marie Barbier, had breast cancer. Dr. Sarrazin's reputation brought her to Québec City. The operation was a success and Sister Barbier was able to return to work and lived for another nineteen years. Anesthesia had not been invented at that time. The archives report that the patient was put to sleep with Gallice wine. The first time chloroform was used as an anesthetic was on January 21, 1848, only two years after the first use of similar procedures by Dr. William Thomas Morton of Boston.[11]

The work done at the Hôtel-Dieu Hospital was considerable. At the request of the civil authorities, abandoned children were taken in. A "porte a tambour" (a special door which contained a revolving wicket or drum,) allowed people to leave children without being seen. More than 1 300 foundlings were thus taken in by the nuns.

In 1693, four nuns from the Hôtel-Dieu accepted the administration of the recently founded Hôpital général.

The Hôtel-Dieu Hospital Museum

A museum, located at 32 rue Charlevoix, testifies to the work of the nuns of the Hôtel-Dieu Hospital and, in a way, to life in Québec from the first years of the French Régime. On display are numerous paintings, including one of Intendant Talon painted by Frère Luc around 1671, and another of Mother Catherine de Saint-Augustin, who was honoured by the founders of the Canadian church and whose beatification procedure has been instituted in Rome. There are also a number of objects there which once belonged to Mme d'Ailleboust who, after the death of her husband, the Governor of New France, lived at the Hôtel-Dieu. Many pieces of old medical equipment, including a scarificator, an instrument used for blood-letting, pilluliers, and chloroform masks are also on display.

The Hôtel-Dieu Museum has preserved many archive documents including a letter from Saint François de Sales and another from Saint Vincent de Paul. On view is a statue of the Virgin Mary, presented in 1738 by an officer who had promised to do so following the miraculous rescue of his ship, La Madeleine. There is also a crucifix which was the object of a sacreligious act. The crime was committed in Montréal, in 1742, and the guilty party was condemned by the Sovereign Council to make honourable amends "nude in a shirt, a rope around the collar, carrying in his hands a burning wax torch weighing two pounds in front of the main door" of the parish church in Montréal and sentenced to five years on a convict ship. Mgr. de

Pontbriand presented the "outraged" crucifix to the Hôtel-Dieu nuns.

The Hôtel-Dieu also hid, at the request of the Premier of Québec, Maurice Duplessis, the "Polish treasures", which were brought to Canada as a security measure at the outbreak of the Second World War. At the end of the war, Premier Duplessis, a Catholic and a notorious anti-Communist, did not want to return the treasures to Poland whose Communist government he refused to recognize. The treasures would finally be returned to Poland during the 1960's.

From the Hôtel-Dieu to rue des Remparts (Ramparts Street)

From the Hôtel-Dieu, you follow rue Charlevoix to rue Hamel and from there proceed to rue des Remparts. Rue Hamel, opened in 1862, is situated on the site of a former cemetery known as the Cemetary of the "Picotés" or pockmarked. The cemetery belonged to the church council of Notre-Dame de Québec and was a burial ground for the poor and "pockmarked" — those who had died of smallpox. When rue Hamel was being built, the remains of these unfortunate people were reburied in Belmont Cemetery, in Sainte-Foy, which, they say, has the reputation of being a cemetery for "the formerly well-to-do". Only on this earth do riches set men apart....

At the corner of Hamel and des Remparts is the "Maison Montcalm" (Montcalm House). Construction of the architectural entity known as maison Montcalm started in 1725, with the building of the main house. Numerous transformations followed. Between 1727 and 1730, two wings were added. Heavily damaged in 1775 during the American attack, the house was restored in 1779-1780. Around 1810, another floor was added to the main house. After 1834, a floor was also added to the wings and, from that time on, each part of the house had its own entrance on rue des Ramparts.

The house has about twenty hearths, wooden panelling, stone walls, fireplaces and vaulted cellars dating back to the French Régime and to the 19th century.

This house was rented to General Montcalm who lived in it from December 1758 to June 1759. In 1775, it was used as a barracks.

During the War of Conquest there were problems with obtaining provisions. The arrival of many soldiers, the lack of farmers, who had been called up to military service, and the lack of communication with France combined to cause shortages. People were therefore advised to kill their horses and to eat them. The "Canadians", being unused to eating horse meat and considering the ownership of a horse or several horses as a sign of prestige, refused to do so. General Montcalm was surprised at this and decided, in order to convince the population, to start eating it himself. "In a letter adressed to the Knight of Lévis, December 4, 1757, he listed the dishes that he had already feasted upon:

"Little horse pâté à l'espagnole
Horse à la mode
Scalloped horse meat
Skewered horse filet with thick pepper-sauce
Horse feet "au gratin"
Horse-tongue stew with onions
Horse frigousse
Smoked horse tongue
Horse cake, like hare cakes."[12]

From maison Montcalm, you now proceed west on rue des Remparts to reach Côte du Palais (Palace Hill).

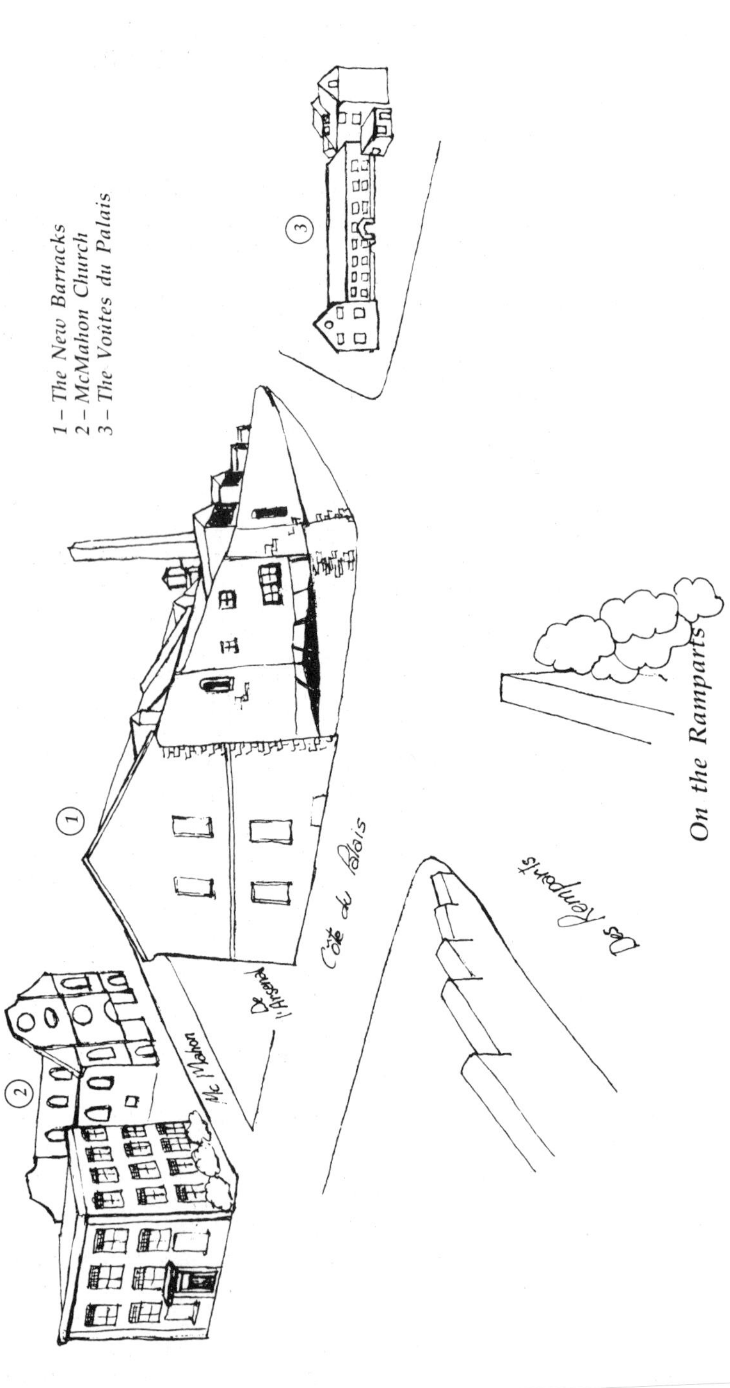

On the Ramparts

4. ON THE RAMPARTS: TOWARD CÔTE DU PALAIS AND THE IRISH QUARTER.

Côte du Palais (Palace Hill)

Rue des Remparts (Rampart St.) leads to Côte du Palais which was first known as the Street of the Poor because it passed through a domain whose revenues were allocated to the needy by the Hôtel-Dieu Hospital. It was also known as rue Saint-Nicolas. In the end, however, it was given the name Côte du Palais (Palace Hill) because it led to the "palace" of the Intendant. The "palace" was actually a combination residence and office.

The Intendance

The creation of the "intendance" or stewardship system, coincided with the reorganization of New France. In 1663, New France was near bancruptcy. Populating the land had proven to be a failure; a mere 2 5000 "Canadiens" were scattered throughout the American continent as opposed to 80 000 American colonists concentrated along the Atlantic seaboard. The necessary reoganization was brought about by King Louis XIV. The Carrignan-Salières regiment was sent to New France to insure the defence of the territory while the reorganization of the colony's political, religious, and economic stuctures, along with the creation of the "intendance", assured a much better framework.

The intendant, known as a "Monseigneur", quickly became one of the most influential personnages in the colony. His jurisdiction included justice, the police, and finances. He presided over sessions of the Soverign Council, directed the administration of the interior and was the "grand argentier" (treasurer) of the colony. Named to his position by the king, the intendant resided in Québec but, like the governor-general, had to spend several months out of each year in Montréal.

Jean Talon was the first intendant actually to take up residence in the colony. Louis Robert de Fortel, the first to be named to the position, never came to Québec. During the course of his two mandates in New France, the first from 1665 to 1668 and the second from 1670 to 1672, Jean Talon assured the reorganization of the colony. He collaborated in the creation of the Sovereign Council, permitted more than 1 500 immigrants to enter the colony and championed a policy of elevated birthrate. A premium of 300 "livres" was given to families with ten children, while families with

Jean Talon

twelve children were accorded 400 "livres". He favoured the sending of several thousand "filles du Roy" (literally, the King's daughters) — orphans who came to find husbands in New France. He also participated in the development of industry, specifically ship building, the manufacture of shoes and the brewing of beer. Talon envisaged a "triangular" commerce between the colony, France, and the French West Indies.

At the time he left Québec in 1672, Talon still owned several properties, one of which was a large house known as the "Brasserie" situated at the corner of Saint-Vallier and Saint-Nicolas streets. This house was purchased by Louis XIV and intended for use by the intendants of New France. Known thereafter as the "Palais Brasserie", it was ravaged by fire in 1713. It was decided, in 1716, to turn the house into a store and prison. The basement walls of this building still exist and are the site of an archeological excavation. In 1715, construction was begun on a new "palace" to the north of the original. This building was later bombarded from the ramparts by the English army in an attempt to dislodge the Americans who had sought refuge there during the siege of Québec in 1775. A section of the vaulted subterranean caverns of the old "palais" still exist today and are known as the "Voûtes du Palais" (Palace Vaults). Acquired by the city of Québec in 1977, this building is now used as an exhibition centre and a site to introduce people to the history of the city. The Voûtes du Palais, situated on rue Saint-Vallier, can be seen from the "New" Barracks whose construction dates from the Conquest. The building of these barracks was begun in 1749 in order to house the soldiers who, during those troubled times, were becoming more and more numerous in Québec. The building is now a part of the architectural ensemble known as Artillery Park, to which we will return a little later.

Côte du Palais (continued)

From rue des Remparts, we now cross Côte du Palais and head toward rue Arsenal. A plaque at the corner of Côte du Palais and Arsenal commemorates Dr. Joseph Painchaud who founded the first Saint-Vincent de Paul Society of Canada on November 12, 1846. Born in 1819, Joseph Painchaud did his classical studies at the Séminaire de Québec. He became a doctor after having had as a teacher, his father, who was a doctor well known for his devotion and self-sacrifice. During a stay in Paris, Painchaud discovered the work of the Saint-Séverin Conferences of the Saint-

Vincent de Paul Society founded in 1833. Upon returning to Canada, Dr. Painchaud established the Society in Canada. In 1851, he was the victim of a shipwreck in the Pacific while on his way to Vancouver. He took refuge in Mexico where, after founding a hospital, he died in about 1886.

An inscription at 14 Côte du Palais recalls the foundation of the Salvation Army in Québec City in 1897. It had existed elsewhere in Canada since 1882. The Salvation Army was founded in London, England in 1865 by William and Catherine Booth whose grandson, Wycliffe Booth, was the National Commander of the Canadian Salvation Army from 1955 to 1964. Membership in this charitable and religious organization now numbers nearly 100 000.

From Côte du Palais to rue McMahon

From Côte du Palais you walk to rue Arsenal and the New Barracks and, from here, to Street by way of tiny rue Carleton. This area was, in the past, the home of the Irish community which was clustered around the church on McMahon and St. Patrick's School which faced it.

The Irish Quarter

The presence of the Irish in Québec dates from 1756. On August 14, 1756, the French army siezed Fort Chouaguen and took some 2 000 prisoners of which a certain number were Irish Catholics. Governor Vaudreuil treated them so well that about fifty of them abandoned the English army to take up residence in Québec. For some time it was hoped that they would join the new recruits of the regular troops, but eventually those in power thought better of it. For the most part, they were employed to work on the fortifications and then were sent to serve in France...

The real Irish immigration began shortly after the Conquest. In 1765, the Québec Gazette reported the first celebration of St. Patrick's Day in Québec. Driven from Ireland by the great famine of the 1830's, many Irish came to Canada under extremely difficult conditions. According to some sources, "of the 100 000 immigrants who left Ireland in 1847, 17 000 perished while crossing the Atlantic; another 5 300 died on Grosse Isle where they were quarantined".[13] In the mid-nineteenth century, the population of the districts known as Champlain and Montcalm was largely Irish. Cap-Blanc, situated at the foot of the cliff to the west of Place Royale, was long considered an Irish bastion. Many of the Irish worked as stevedors. They had a virtual monopoly in this work due to the strength of their union, but this was quickly contested by Francophone workers who, in turn formed a rival association. The resolution of this rivalry was not achieved until the end of the century.

At that time, living conditions in the Irish quarter were pitiful, at best. Poverty as well as epidemics added to the general insecurity of the area. The area was ravaged by fire, and more than once rue Champlain was buried under snow and landslides. It was said that artillery fire aimed at targets on the river ice might have been the cause of the landslides and the exercises were stopped.

In 1830, there were 7 000 Irish in Québec which had a total population of 32 000. In 1870, the Irish community still constituted more than one fifth of the population of the city.

When they arrived in this country, the Irish Catholics made use of churches constructed by French-speaking Catholics for their religious services. Thus, Notre-Dame-des-Victoires (Our Lady of Victories) Church long served both communities. The construction of St. Patrick's Church on rue McMahon put an end to this practice.

Until the 1950's, this church remained the focal point of the Irish community in Québec and, in a larger sense, of all English-speaking Catholics, who had, in 1866, obtained permisson to become members of the congregation regardless of their parish of residence. Mass was celebrated here until St. Patrick's Day, March 17, 1958. A new church, built on the Grande Allée, and other new buildings nearer the heart of the Irish community, eventually took over from the rue McMahon church. The name McMahon brings to mind the memory of the first curé to serve there. The rue McMahon church was finally closed in 1959 and, later, burnt down. The presbytery, situated at 79 rue Saint-Stanislas, is a good example of English neo-classical architecture. It was designed by Goodlate Richardson Browne and built in 1854-55. St. Patrick's School, situated across from the church was built in 1883 and closed in 1919.

Toward Artillery Park

From the old Irish church we now go up rue McMahon toward Artillery Park until we reach Dauphine Redoubt.

1 – Dauphine Redoubt
2 – The Arsenal
3 – The Officers' Quarters
4 – The Church of the Soeurs de la Charité

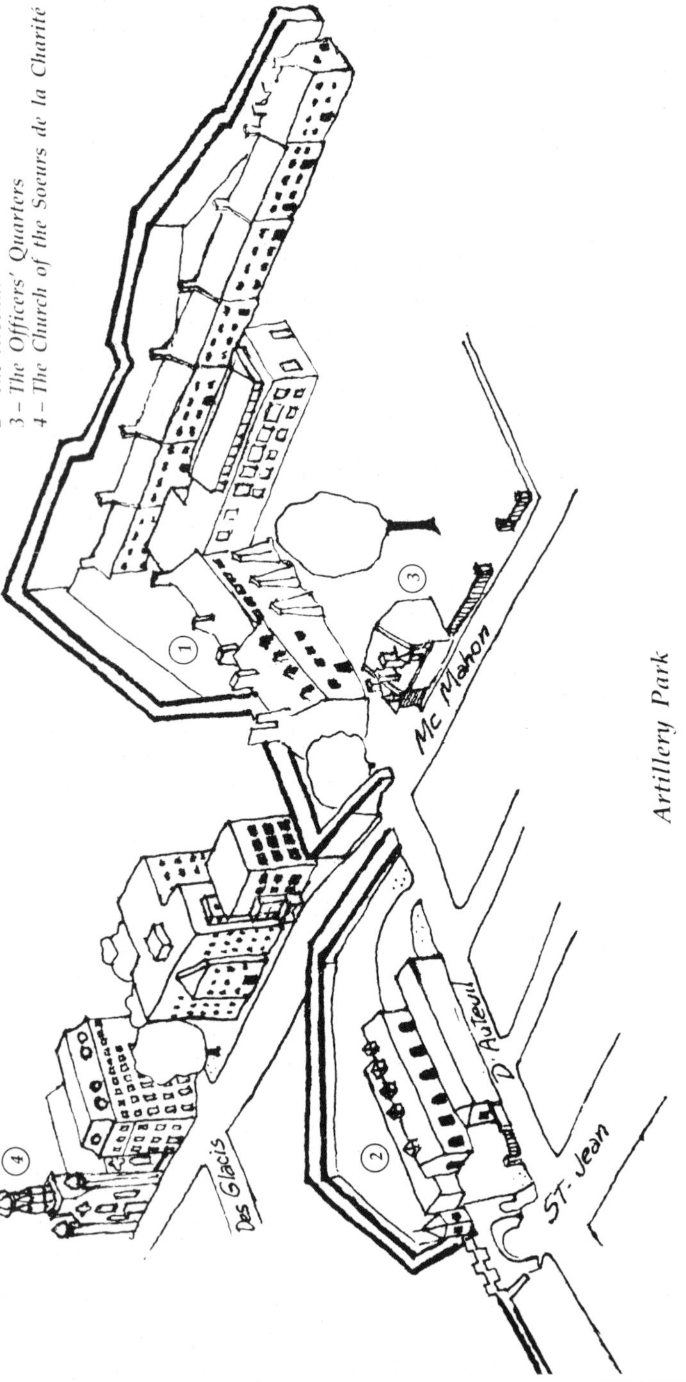

5. ARTILLERY PARK

Historical Background

Artillery Park is made up of two sections, one military, the other civilian. The fortifications, foundry, gun carriage shed, new barracks, Dauphine Redoubt, officers' residence, arsenal workshop, warehouse, and guardhouse make up the military section. The civilian sector is made up of approximately ten buildings which include warehouses, houses, and St. Patrick's School. Artillery Park covers about six percent of Old Québec and is, by and large, situated in the area bordered by the Ramparts, Saint-Jean and D'Auteuil streets and Côte du Palais. Over the course of history, Artillery Park has seen numerous modifications and been put to a variety of uses.

The stategic value of the site was recognized very early on, and it was here that people fled in times of attack from the valley of the rivière Saint-Charles. In 1690, the first defensive works were begun and were added to by Beaucourt in 1693. In 1697, a surrounding wall was constructed but was replaced, in 1712, by a low masonry wall. This wall became part of a group of walls which was to have included five fortified towers. The Treaty of Utrecht, signed in 1713, brought peace and an end to work on the fortifications. The Dauphine Redoubt, which is the second oldest military building in Québec (the oldest being the redoubt located inside the present citadel) is the result of this construction. In 1748, Chaussegros de Levy had the Redoubt transformed into a barracks as a part of the new defensive works. The arrival of numerous military personnel at the time of the Conquest necessitated the construction of new barracks between 1749 and 1754. This building, which is 175 × 15 metres (525 × 45), was the longest such construction in New France. It is three storeys high.

The Park retained its military character after the Treaty of Paris. The site contained the headquarters of the Royal Artillery stationed in Québec. New buildings were added to the site. In 1818, the old bakery was converted into officers' lodgings. This building, which is about fifty feet long by seventeen feet wide, is located on rue McMahon near the Dauphine Redoubt. The guardhouse was built in 1832. After the departure of the English garrison in 1871, Artillery Park became a cartridge factory. The engine block and rolling mill were installed in the new barracks which had been destroyed by fire in 1857 and reconstructed between 1898 and 1901. The interior court of the old parade ground was transformed into a shell factory, and a foundry was added in 1902 on the old power magazine emplacement. This change of "vocation" considerably altered the architecture of the Park which, in 1901, became the Federal Arsenal. The expansion of the cartridge factory continued into the twentieth century, reaching its height during the two World Wars.

The Côte du Palais installations quickly became insufficient, and, in 1939, new factories were built at Valcartier. In 1940, a third cartridge plant was set up in the old workshops of the Canadian National Railway in Saint-Malo district. At the height of the conflict, the Federal Arsenal was one of the principal employers in the region with more than 14 000 employees, of which 2 000 worked at the Côte du Palais site. With the return to peace-time, the Saint-Malo factory was closed, and more and more of the production was concentrated at the Valcartier plant. The Côte du Palais installation was finally closed in November 1964.

The 1970's signalled a new beginning for Artillery Park. The federal government, which had owned the buildings since 1871, undertook a restoration programme and the Park became, along with Place Royale, an important centre of activity in Old Québec. An interpretation centre was set up in the old foundry where visitors can admire a scale-model of Québec which is the work of Jean-Baptiste Duberger, who was a land surveyor in the office of the Royal Engineers of Québec, and John By, who was an engineer working in the city.

The Duberger Model

The Duberger Model faithfully reproduces the topographical data of the city and its physical layout in 1808. Begun on what seems to have been the personal initiative of Duberger and By, the scale model took on, with time, a more official character. At the beginning of the 19th century, war was a constant threat, and numerous military constructions were undertaken. The model, which demonstrated clearly the need for any work to be done, became an important working tool.

Governor Craig sent the model to England in 1810, and it remained there until 1908. When it was returned to Canada, it was placed in the Federal Archives and returned to Artillery Park in 1979.

Originally, the model was constructed on a scale of 1/300 and measured 6.15 × 10 metres. Around 1860, the western portion, which had likely extended as far as Bougainville and Brown Streets, was cut off to create the present limits of the model.

The maker of the work was long in doubt as a result of a letter written by John By in 1811 to the inspector general of fortifications in which he minimized the work of Duberger and accorded himself all of the credit. The truth was later established and By and Duberger are now recognized as co-authors of the model.

The Sisters of Charity

From rue McMahon, we can see the buildings belonging to the Sisters of Charity to the west on rue Richelieu. The chapel, the work of Charles Baillairgé, deserves comment. Destroyed by fire for the first time in 1854, it was reconstructed two years later. In 1914, it was again destroyed by fire and rebuilt.

The Sisters of Charity, founded by Marguerite d'Youville in Montréal and established in Québec City in 1849 are better known as the Gray Nuns.

This nickname dates from the French Regime but came into popular usage at a time when Montréal was divided into two camps over the subject of a hospital directed by the Charon brothers. The administration of this institution had been disastrous, and trouble erupted over who would take over. One side urged that this be handled by men, while the other wanted a female administration (the Sisters of Charity).

When it became evident that the women would prevail, partisans of the opposing camp spread malicious stories about the good sisters. They were accused of drunkenness and of selling alcohol to the Amerindians. It is as a result of this slanderous gossip that the Sisters were derisively named the "Grey Nuns", a name given in many parts of France because of the colour of thir habits but taken, in Québec, in a completely different sense.

From Artillery Park to Rue D'Auteuil

After having visited the principal buildings of Artillery Park — Dauphine Redoubt, the officers' lodgings, and the interpretation centre — you now proceed to rue D'Auteuil and the neighbouring ramparts.

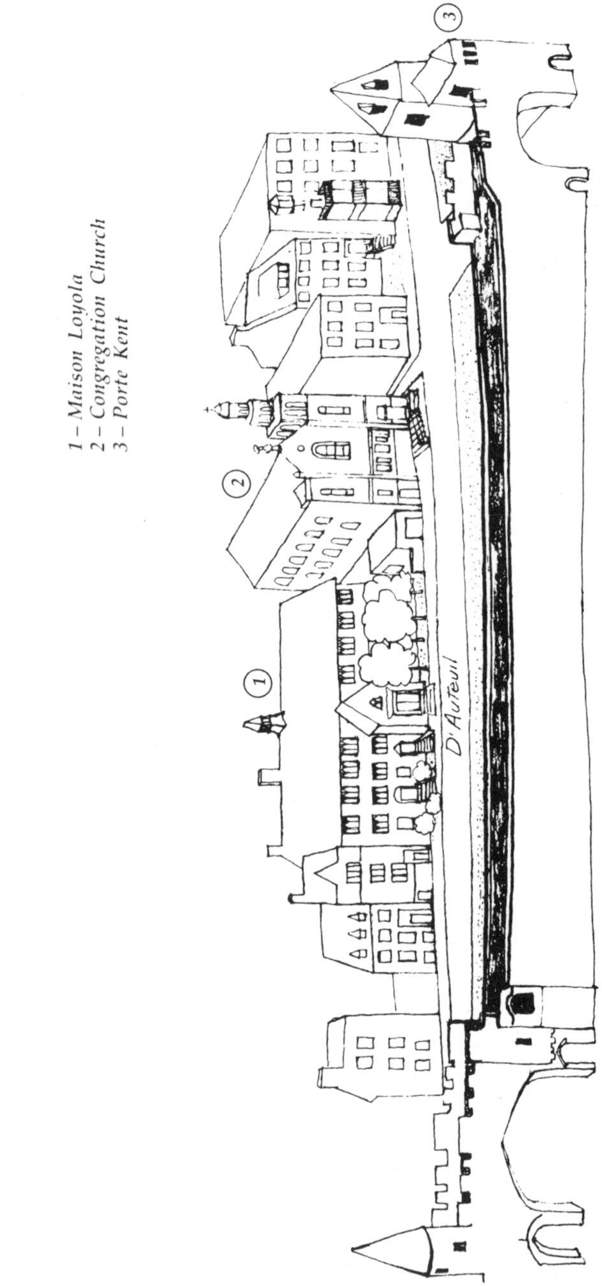

1 – Maison Loyola
2 – Congregation Church
3 – Porte Kent

Rue D'Auteuil

6. D'AUTEUIL: A SECOND RAMPART

Rue D'Auteuil extends from rue McMahon to the Citadel. Part of the street was once known as rue Dalhousie. The name was changed in April 1876. Rue D'Auteuil was named in honour of Joseph Ruette D'Auteuil de Monceaux and François-Madeleine Fortuné Ruette D'Auteuil, his son. Both were Attornies-general of the Sovereign Council of New France. The street, with its stone buildings forms a kind of second rampart. Several houses which have, without a doubt, great historical importance are found there.

Maison Loyola and Congregation Church

Maison Loyala, 29-35 rue D'Auteuil, is the oldest neogothic building in the city. Built in 1822-1824 with one storey added later, the building was officially acquired in 1830 by the Anglican bishop and made into a "National School", the first school of the Anglican faith in Québec City. The Jesuits bought the institution in 1904.

This transaction, which took place in an era when ecumenicalism was as yet unheard of, may seem quite strange, some people saw it as a divine intervention. A little girl from the Catholic community had the idea of burying a Saint Joseph medallion on the "National School" grounds. The gesture, in spite of its candor and simplicity, was the reason for the transaction.

Next to the Maison Loyola, the church of the Congregation of Notre-Dame de Québec was built in 1818 according to plans drawn up by François Baillairgé. The church has since been enlarged and its structure modified several times. The last restoration dates from 1931. The men the Congregation of Notre-Dame-de-Québec, a lay association having special devotion to the Holy Virgin, was founded in Québec on Feburary 14, 1657, following a Jesuit tradition recognized cononically by Pope Gregory XIII, in 1584. The Congregation had its first meetings in the main building of the former Collège des Jésuites. In 1818, it was officially established on rue D'Auteuil. It was administrated by the Parish clergy until 1850, the year the Jesuits returned to Québec. In 1839, the members of the congregation who came from the Lower Town, finding the location distant and no doubt thinking that there was little affinity between themselves and the "monsieurs" of the Upper Town, founded, in Saint-Roch, their own congregation. Their church, built in 1853, and enlarged by the choir, in 1875, later became the parish church of Notre-Dame-de-Jacques Cartier.

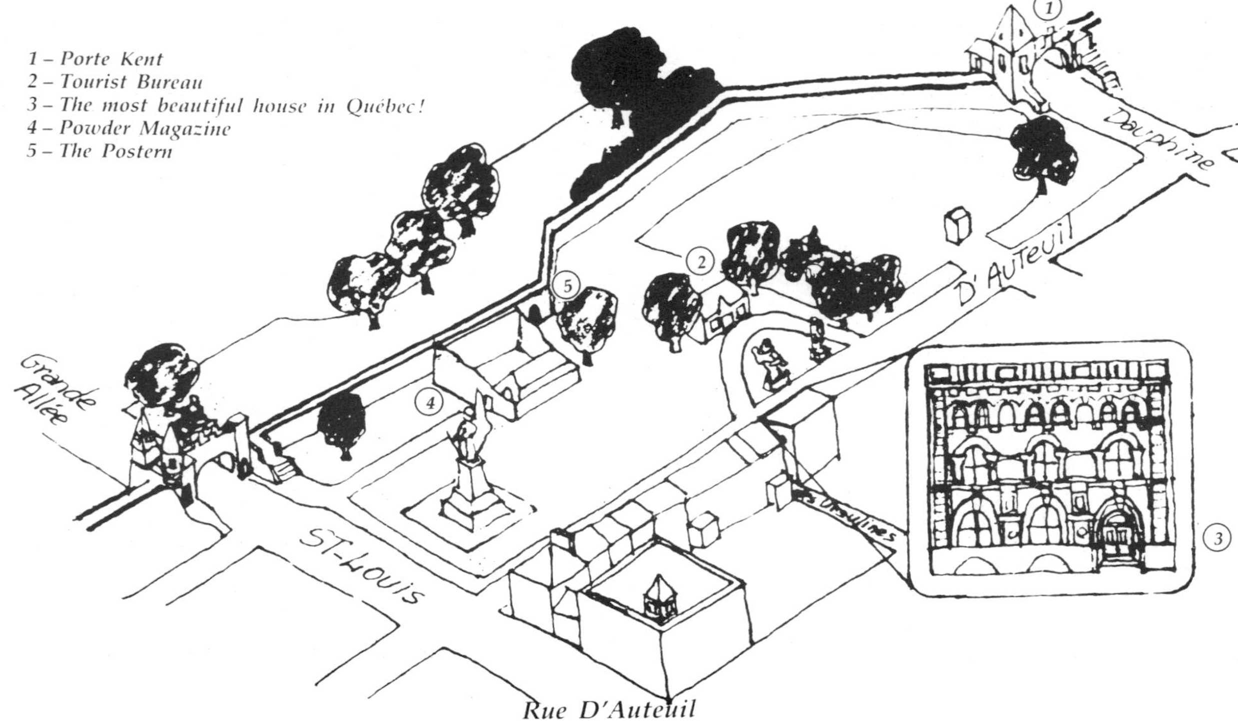
1 – Porte Kent
2 – Tourist Bureau
3 – The most beautiful house in Québec!
4 – Powder Magazine
5 – The Postern
Dauphine
D'Auteuil
Grande Allée
ST-LOUIS
Rue D'Auteuil

The Congregation's society is less flourishing today than it was in the past. The first prefect of the Congregation was Charles de Lauzon, a gentleman from Charny, who was, at that time, replacing his father as Governor of New France. In 1900, Judge A.-B. Routhier, a member since 1891, was the guest speaker at the celebrations which marked the two hundred and fiftieth anniversary of the founding of the society.

Without a doubt, the members of the congregation on this occasion remembered the sacriligious theft by Chambers and his gang, February 9, 1835. Breaking into the Church, they stole two ciboria, (vessels containing the host) a statuette, a crucifix and six candelabra. This theft was not their only crime. When they were arrested in 1836, they were charged with more than nine misdeeds, including the murder of a lighthouse-keeper. After their sacrilege at the Congregation Church, the thieves went to the Norris family home, in Broughton in the Beauce, to melt down the stolen objects. Cecilia Connor, a family servant, intrigued by the arrival of the visitors, watched her employer's comings and goings carefully. She surprised him, with Chambers and his gang, melting the stolen objects in a "cabane à sucre" (sugar cabin). Outraged at seeing a statuette of the Virgin Mary melted and transformed into ordinary money, Cécilia Connor denounced the thieves. Following long proceedings and with the help of a former accomplice, Chambers was found guilty and sentenced to death. The day before his execution Chambers' punishement was commuted and he was deported to Australia. In Québec, people forgot the affair. Robert Chambers, brother of the famous thief, was able to be elected as mayor of Québec in 1878, without anyone reminding him of the wrong doings of his "illustrious" relative.

Porte Kent

Porte Kent was built to the west of rue D'Auteuil around 1880. Named in the honour of the Duke of Kent, Queen Victoria's father, who visited Québec City at the end of the 18th century, Porte Kent was part of the improvements made by Lord Dufferin at the end of the last century. This gate replaced a postern, a type of door concealed in the fortification wall.

The Tourist Bureau on the Esplanade

The Tourism and Congress Service-centre for the Urban Community of Québec City (Tourist Bureau) is a located at

The 30th Carnaval de Québec, 1984.
(The Carnaval Committee)

60 rue D'Auteuil. Between the tourist centre and the public parking lot, there is an area reserved for the coachmen of the city, the starting point for a memorable tour in a horse-drawn calèche around the streets of Québec. Worth noticing is the totem pole in front of the building, which is the work of sculptor Mungo Martin. It was given to the city of Québec by British Columbia, one of the ten Canadian provinces, on the occasion of the 26th Annual Congress on Canadian Tourism Association, September 22, 1958. A monument representing "Bonhomme Carnaval", located across from the tourist centre is a reminder of the importance of the Québec City Winter Carnival.

The first carnivals were held during the French regime. The inhabitants of New France, according to an old French custom, celebrated the carnival or Mardi-gras by organizing festivities. At the end of the last century, the Winter Carnival attracted a large crowd. An ice palace, and slides were built, and sports and social activities were organized. Then, with the passage of time, the tradition died out. In the mid

The ice palace of the 30th Carnaval de Québec
(The Carnaval Committee)

1950's, the city's businessmen, noticing a considerable decline in the number of tourists visiting the city during the winter, proposed holding a carnival. Since then, the Carnival has become a major tourist attraction which contributes to the economic well-being of the city.

Parc de l'Esplanade

The grounds between the walls and rue D'Auteuil are called parc de l'Esplanade. First a pasture, the spot became, after the construction of the walls and Citadel around 1830, a military exercise ground. The spot replaced Place d'armes, which, up to that time, had been used for that purpose. Worth noticing is the powder magazine against wall, which was built at the end of the 19th century. The powder magazine, owned by the Canadian government, is now an information centre. An explanation of the city's defense system completes the services offered by the Artillery information centre, whose principal objectives are to explain the living conditions of soldiers in Québec City and the role of the Arsenal.

The Most Beautiful House in Québec...

At the corner of rue des Ursulines (the narrowest street in Québec City), and rue D'Auteuil, is it is said, one of the most beautiful houses in Québec. Built around 1872 by the Honourable Thomas McGreevy, Parliamentary advisor, the house was first rented to an Anglican bishop in 1892 who later bought it. It became the official place of residence of the Anglican bishop of the diocese of Québec. A bronze plaque, hung in the front hall, bears the name "See House" just as in all the other residences of Anglican bishops in the world. The house has four floors, nineteen rooms, and fifteen fireplaces, each built with a different kind of marble. It has an immense staircase lit by a shaft of light, mahogany and oak panelling, a ballroom, which was converted into three large bedrooms, servants quarters and a finished basement. In 1971, the Anglican bishop decided to leave the house which was too spacious and too difficult to maintain.[15] The building now contains a youth hostel.

From rue D'Auteuil to the Legislative Complex

From rue D'Auteuil, you cross Parc de l'Esplanade and go through the Postern across from the former residence of the Anglican bishop. From there, you make your way to the legislative complex. The elbow-shaped postern permitted defenders to come back into the enclosure without being open to enemy fire.

1 – *The Parlement*
2 – *The Mercier Monument*
3 – *The Drill Hall*
4 – *The Short-Wallick Monument*
5 – *Anima "G"*
6 – *The chapel of the mother house of the Soeurs du Bon-Pasteur*
7 – *The F.X. Garneau Monument*

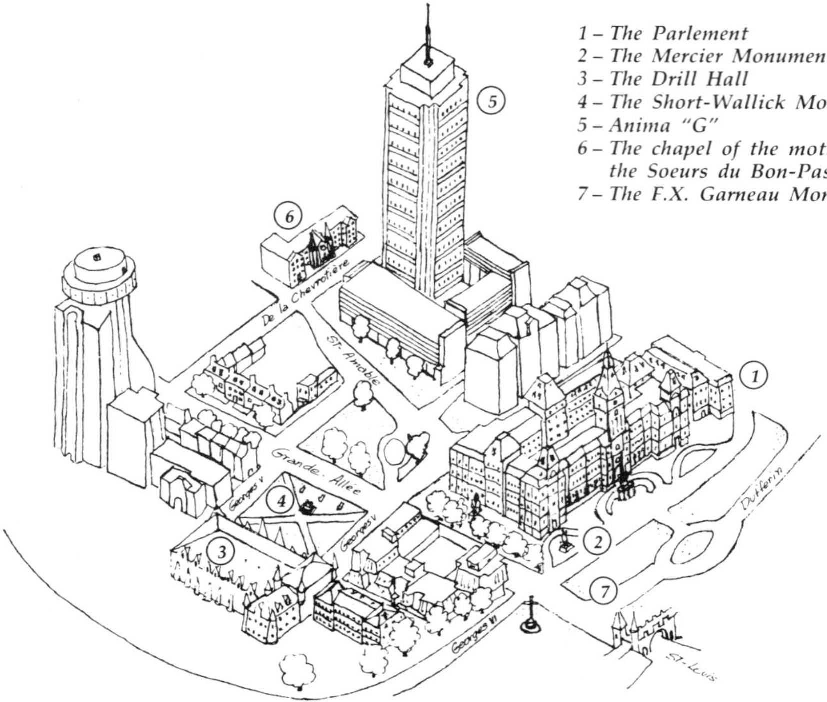

The Legislative Complex

7. THE LEGISLATIVE COMPLEX OR THE HISTORY OF PARLIAMENTARY GOVERNMENT

The Assemblée Nationale Building (The Legislative Building)

The Assemblée Nationale was built in 1877 and 1884. The cornerstone of the portico at the main entrance to the building was laid on June 17, 1884 by the Lieutenant-Governor of the Province of Québec, Theodore Robitaille. According to Ernest Gagnon, the land on which the Assemblée Nationale was built had once been a part of the Saint-François fief, the first concession of which goes back to 1646. The surface area of the land was 23 399 square metres. The federal government purchased the land and, then, later sold it to the province on August 14, 1876, for 15 000$. It was called "Garrison Cricket Field" at that time. The government of Québec also bought a piece of land from the city which was turned into the Allée de la Fontaine (Fountain Drive). The supervision of the construction was entrusted to the architects J.B. Dérome and Pierre Gauvreau, and the plans were the responsibility of Eugène-Étienne Pascal Taché, former Prime Minister of Canada from 1864 to 1867. The building, of French Renaissance style, forms a quadrilateral with each side measuring approximately 100 metres (300 feet). The central tower is a little more than 50 metres (172 feet) high.

Different buildings were subsequently added to the central building in 1915, the Pamphile-Lemay Building housing the National Library; the Honoré-Mercier and André-Laurendeau Buildings, in 1925 and 1932, respectively; and Annex E completed the complex in 1934. In the 1960's and 1970's, the complex was enlarged with the addition of Buildings G and other buildings either built or bought along the Grande Allée or elsewhere in the area.

E.-E. Taché, the architect, designed the front of the Assemblée Nationale Building as a memorial to the history of the Province of Québec and Canada. It was reported that Taché had been hurt by the comment of Lord Durham who had come to the Canadian colony to undertake an inquiry following the 1837 Rebellion. The latter had stated that "Canadians were a people without any history." Taché wanted to prove him wrong. The numerous monuments, the many coats of arms carved in the stone, and the expression "Je me souviens" ("I remember") engraved in the main portico of the building served as an eloquent reply to Lord Durham. "Je me souviens" became the official motto of the province on February 9, 1883. The fountain was dedicated, according to Taché's own words, to "the proud aboriginal tribes of Canada." The sculptures entitled "Le pêcheur à la Nigoque" and "La Halte dans la Forêt" are both the work of Philippe Hébert. They bring to mind the first inhabitants of the country.

History is as much present inside as outside the building. Blazons and old coats of arms are finely carved in the mahogony. In the large entrance hall, we find the emblems of the different nations that have played a role in the history of Québec. The stairway leads to the two chambers — the Salon Bleu (The Blue Room) and the Salon Rouge (the Red Room).

The fresco on the ceiling of the Salon Bleu illustrates the great moments in the history of the province which is divided into three main periods: the French Régime (1534-1760), the British Régime (1760-1867), and the period since Confederation (1867). This painting is the work of Charles Huot, who was in his 70's at the time. In spite of his age, he had to work lying on his back three hours a day. It took him more than four years to complete the task.

Charles Huot was also responsible for another painting, this one representing the debate held on January 21, 1793, concerning the status of the French language in the Québec Parliament. He also did a painting illustrating the Sovereign Council of New France which is found in the Salon Rouge, usually the site of the meetings of the Assemblée Nationale committees. The painter died at the age of 75 in 1930, before completing the work. The artists Neilson and Maillard finished it.

The Beginnings of Parliamentary Government

The parliamentary system in Québec dates from the end of the 19th century. By the Constitutional Act of 1791, England divided her Canadian colony into two provinces — Upper Canada (Ontario) and Lower Canada (Québec) — each with its own government and the eight to elect its own legislative assembly. Québec was chosen the capital of Lower Canada and York (Toronto), of Upper Canada.

In 1792, Québécois elected their first members, The former episcopal palace, located in parc Montmorency, was chosen as the site of the first legislative assembly.

In 1841, the two former colonies created in 1791 were reunited into a single colony, the United Province of Canada. Kingston was chosen as the new capital, but the choice was not unanimous. In 1844, Parliament was moved to

The Parlement du Québec:
Central Building (1884)

Montréal where it remained until the aftermath of the annexation crisis of 1849. It was decided to continue the session in Toronto and, then, to alternate with Québec every four years. The episcopal palace once again became the seat of Parliament.

In 1854, fire destroyed the building and the members had to find a new site. The couvent of the Sisters of Charity on rue Saint-Olivier was rented. Because this building had also just been damaged by fire, restoration work was begun using Charles Baillargé's plans. Three months later, the site was destroyed by another fire. Parliament was temporarily moved to the Académie Saint-Louis on rue Saint-Louis and, then, to the former courthouse near Place d'Armes. In 1856, the system of alternation began. Parliament was shifted to Toronto. During the four-year absence, new legislative buildings were built in Québec. In 1859, a new building was put up in parc Montmorency according to the plans of F.P. Rubidge. It was the seat of Parliament from 1860 to 1864. This building was destroyed by fire in 1883. In the meantime, Ottowa was chosen as national capital. In 1867, Québec became the provincial capital. The legislature first sat in the building in parc Montmorency, then, from 1884, in the present location.

Québec: One of Ten Provinces

Québec is one of ten Canadian provinces. Canada, itself, is a federation of provinces which is governed by two levels of government: the provincial level which is made up of the ten provincial governments, and the federal government. The jurisdictions of the two levels of government are spelled out in the Canadian constitution whose central article is the British North America Act. Generally speaking, the provincial governments have jurisdiction over affairs of civilian society such as education and health, whereas the federal government is responsible for international affairs or any such area which involves Canadians as a whole.

The limits of jurisdiction between the two levels of government are not always clear. Whereas a rich province might have "decentralist" tendancies, a poor province might prefer a more "centralist" policy, leaving to the federal government the cost of services which the province could not otherwise afford to offer.

Historically, the government of Québec, due to its cultural and economic distinction, has favoured a "decentralist" constitutional policy.

In 1890, just a few short years after the creation of Canada, Québec Premier, Honoré Mercier, whose outlook was decidedly "provincialist", convened the first conference of provincial premiers.

Canada is a constitutional monarchy. In principle, the representative of the sovereign, (the Governor-General at the federal level and the Lieutenant-Governor in each province), holds the power. In practice, however, the power belongs to the leader of either the party holding a majority of the seats or a coalition of the majority of elected deputies. An election must be held at least once every five years and each election results in a new legislature. At the beginning of each legislature, the deputies elect a president who is responsible for the direction and control of debates. Each legislature is divided into many sessions of variable length — usually about seven months between the convocation and the prorogation of the Legislative Assembly which, in Québec, in 1968, became known as the Assemblée Nationale.

Every projected law proposed to the assembly by the government must succeed in passing a series of three steps known as "readings". On the first reading, the law is tabled with no debate. At the second reading, the principle of the law is voted on and, at the third reading, after having been studied in commission, the projected law is put to the vote of the members. Every projected law which has passed this vote in the Assemblée Nationale must receive the official sanction of the lieutenant-governor before being passed into law.

The Mercier Monument

A monument situated to the north of Grande Allée and facing the Parliament recalls the memory of Honoré Mercier and is the work of French sculptor Paul Chevré. It was officially unveiled on June 25, 1912. The ceremony coincided with the first French language congress and the different delegations came to pay homage to this great man. The monument shows Mercier with his hand extended and cynics claim that it was, in fact, erected to the memory of calèche drivers waiting for their tips!

Journalist, lawyer, politician and premier (1887-1892), Mercier settled, during the course of his mandate, the question of Jesuit properties, organized libraries, founded night schools, promoted a "natalist" policy by granting free land to fathers with twelve or more children and favoured colonization. Profoundly nationalist, Mercier rose to power by provoking the popular indignation against those respon-

sible for the hanging of Louis Riel. As previously mentioned, he also convened the first interprovincial conference.

The last years of his life were shadowed by accusations. Removed from office by Lieutenant-Governor Angers who dominated the federal politicians, Mercier was forced to testify before the Court of Assizes. He was exonerated by the jury but was unable to accept the personal affront. He died two years later on October 30, 1894.

Grande Allée

The street known as Grande Allée extends from the porte Saint-Louis to Avenue des Érables (Maples Ave.). The name Grande Allée dates from the French Regime when it was, indeed, a veritable "allée" — a tree lined road.

With the construction of the present "Hôtel du Gouvernement" at the end of the nineteenth century, Grande Allée became one of the most "select" streets in the city, thus taking precedence over rue Saint-Louis which had previously been important because of the Chateau Haldimand, the residence of the Governor and the proximity to parc Montmorency, the site of the earlier parliamentary buildings.

In 1900, one could not live on Grande Allée simply because one wanted to do so. It was necessary to be one of the "beautiful people" of the day. There is a story told of one wealthy French-Canadian industrialist who had to ask permission of Louis-Alexandre Taschereau, premier of Québec from 1926-36, whose four storey, forty-two room house was situated at 425 Grande Allée, before moving onto the street.

At the beginning of the century, one journalist described Grande Allée as "a river of light, an exaggerated and insolent light which sweeps under the porte Saint-Louis, laps against the Garrision Club and creates a transition between the past and the present. Ministers, deputies and legislative counsellors live or stay there. Political clubs are located there and the great families have their homes".

But Grande Allée has not always had such a good reputation. At the end of the seventeenth century, hangman Jean Rattier lived there. In the early days of the colony, it was often difficult to find a hangman. When this happened, the guilty man's sentence was commuted on the condition that he fill the post, himself. The first hangman to be officially named in New France was a town-crier from Montréal, found guilty of a "crime against nature" in 1648. Jean Rattier also benefited from this arrangement. Accused of murder, he escaped the noose and became the official hangman of

New France in 1690. However, Jean Rattier was not at the end of his problems. In 1695, his wife Marie Rivière and daughter Marie Charlotte were arrested and charged with theft. Thus, the honest folk of Québec were treated to the unusual spectacle of a women put in the iron collar by her own husband.

Nowadays, Grande Allée has changed its vocation. Along with rue Saint-Jean, it constitutes Québec "by night" and has maintained its "select" position. Those who have succeeded and those who are still optimistic have their rendezvous there. From numerous terrasses, people watch pedestrians, no doubt recalling the story of "La Corriveau" who, one day, was forced to walk up Grande Allée as far as "Buttes-à-Nepveu" (near Taché Street) to be hanged.

At the end of the winter of 1763, Joseph Corriveau and his daughter Marie-Josephte of Saint-Vallier were arrested and accused of the murder of Louis-Étienne Dodier, Marie-Josephte's second husband. The trial was held in Québec at the Ursuline convent. After many days of hearings, the father was condemned to death and his daughter, found quilty of complicity, was to be flogged and branded. The day before his execution, Joseph Corriveau, who was innocent and had allowed himself to be condemned to save his daughter, realized that, it he persisted in his silence, he "would be, in the words of his confessor, his own murderer for which there would be no hope of pardon in the hereafter."[16] The next day he retracted his story and his daughter had to admit to the crime. She was condemned to be hanged at "Buttes-à-Nepveu". To make an example of her, her body was placed in a cage designed to fit the human form which was then hung from a tree at a crossroads in Lauzon. Purchased some years later, the cage became part of the attractions of the celebrated Barnum Circus.

The Military Drill Hall (Manège Militaire)

The Military Drill Hall is situated on the south side of Grande Allée. Constructed in 1885 according to plans by architect E.E. Taché, the building was put to both military and civilan use. Provincial exhibitions were held there. The exhibition or exercise arena measures approximately 80 × 30 metres (260 × 90′) and is not supported by a single column. The exterior of the building is made of stone. The "barbacane" windows on the ground floor and the windows which mount to the copper roof are worth noticing. The Drill Hall houses the museum of the Québec "Voltigeurs".

This light infantry regiment, founded on March 7, 1862 is one of the most prestigious in Québec.

The Short-Wallick Monument

The Short-Wallick Monument across from the Drill Hall is dedicated to the memory of two members of the Québec garrison who were tragically killed at the end of the last century. During the night of May 15, 1889, a terrible fire broke out in the Saint-Sauveur district of the Lower Town. More than 400 houses were consumed by flames. In an attempt to stop the catastrophe, it was decided to destroy some buildings. A barrel of gunpowder placed in one of the buildings did not go off. Short and Wallick went to check; but, before they could finish their inspection, the powder exploded. They were both killed. On November 12, 1891, the people of Québec put up a monument to honour the two men. It is the work of Phillippe Hébert. At the top, there are busts of the heroes; at the foot of the monument, a women representing Québec City renders them homage in the name of the citizens of the city.

"Anima G"

Édifice G stands to the north of the Grande Allée across from the *Drill Hall*. To get there, you follow rue de la Chevrotière. In order to exploit the magnificent view of the city from the top of the building, an observation floor was created.

The Chapel of the Soeurs du Bon-Pasteur

The Chapel of the Soeurs du Bon-Pasteur is located a few steps from Complexe G at 1080 rue de la Chevrotière. It was classified as an historical monument on October 8, 1975. It was built between 1866 and 1868 according to the plans of Charles Baillairgé. The facade, which was rebuilt in 1909, is the work of the architect Berlinguet. The building's dimensions give it its uniqueness. The chapel contains many precious objects including an 1869 painting of the Virgin Mary by Plamondon and a tabernacle designed by Levasseur in 1739. The sisters obtained this last item from the parish of Lotbinière in exchange for some of their own paintings. The Congregation of the Soeurs du Bon-Pasteur was founded in Québec City by Marie Fitzbach and was canonically established on February 2, 1856.

The François Xavier Garneau Monument

This monument, located near the porte Saint-Louis across from the Assemblée Nationale, was officially unveiled on October 10, 1912. It was created by the French sculptor, Paul Chevré, to honour the national historian of the Province of Québec. His masterwork, a three-volume history of Canada entitled *Histoire du Canada,* was published in 1845, 1846, and 1848. For the first time, French Canadians were shown the greatness of their history. Garneau, like Taché, the architect of the Parliament building, wanted to respond to Lord Durham who felt that the French Canadians were a people without any history. The historian exercised several functions including city clerk. He died in 1866 at the age of 57. His memory is honoured throughout the city. Street monuments, and institutions, including a college bearing his name, are named after him, The Monument François Xavier Garneau was offered to the Government of Québec by the Honourable G.E. Amyot, legislative counsellor and a relative of the great historian.

From Colline Parlementaire (Parliament Hill) to Rue Saint-Louis

After a tour of the colline parlementaire and a stop at one of the many café-terrasses of the Grande Allée, you head toward the Old City until you reach the porte Saint-Louis.

1 – Porte Saint-Louis
2 – The Monument aux Braves de la Guerre des Boers
3 – The Citadel
4 – The Maison Sewell
5 – The Garrison Club

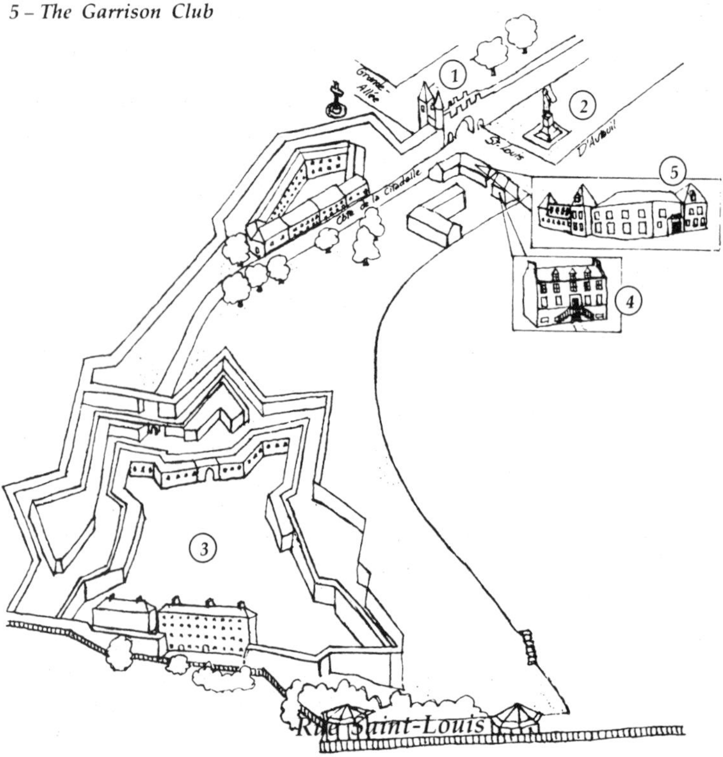

8. RUE SAINT-LOUIS

The Grande Allée of the Past

Rue Saint-Louis is one of the oldest in Québec City. The name was chosen by Governor de Montmagny in honour if King Louis XIII of France. This street was one of the most fashionable ones before the construction of the Assemblée Nationale in 1884. It led to Place d'Armes and parc Montmorency which, at that time were the focal point of political activity in the colony. According to Joseph Bouchette, surveyor-general of Lower Canada, rue Saint-Louis in 1815 was "by far and away the most beautiful part of the town. Most of the principal members of Parliament, as well as the leading figures of society, lived on the street. Several of the houses are modern and very beautiful."[17]

The porte Saint-Louis

The first porte Saint-Louis was put up in 1693 at the same time as the first porte Saint-Jean. Thereafter, it was demolished and reconstructed several times. The present gate dates back to 1878 and was one of Lord Dufferin's projects. It was designed by W.H. Lynn according to the plans of Charles Baillairgé.

The Monument aux Braves de la guerre des Boers (Monument to the Courageous Soldiers of the Boer War)

This monument was unveiled before the Governor-General of Canada, Sir Grey, the Prince of Battenberg, and several British officers on August 15, 1905. The lines engraved on the monument were composed by Reverend M.F.G. Scott.

The Citadel

Côte de la Citadelle (Citadel Hill) is a few feet from the porte Saint-Louis and leads to the fortress of Québec. Samuel de Champlain and Jean Bourdon first had the idea of building a citadel in 1634. In 1716, an engineer, Chaussegros de Léry, proposed the construction of a defensive installation and drew up the plans in 1720. The citadel had still not been built at the time of the Conquest. A powder magazine built in the 1750's and the Cap-aux-Diamants redoubt dating from 1693 were the only structures on the heights of Québec. After the Conquest, different projects were submitted, but none were carried out. Around 1790, a bit of excavation work was done, and this constituted a supposedly temporary citadel. The present structure was built between the years 1820 and 1830 according to the plans of Colonel Durnford. The star-shaped construction is in the Vauban style.

Notice that the cannons are facing the streets leading to the Citadel; this was done to beat back any attack coming from inside the walls.

The Citadel is open to visitors. A very popular tourist attraction is the changing of the guard which takes place daily.

The museum is found in a former French powder magazine built around 1750. It is dedicated to the military history of Canada, and, in particular, to the Royal 22nd Regiment, created in 1914 and one of the most prestigious French-speaking regiments. The Museum contains different war trophies — medals, decorations, uniforms, documents, maps, and several very precious objects including two pistols once belonging to General Wolfe and an old French musket dating from 1693.

The official Québec City residence of Canada's Governor-General is located in the Citadel. The building was damaged by fire a few years ago; however, it has been renovated, and the Queen's representative in Canada will once again be able to stay there in 1984.

The chapel of the Citadel, located in a former powder magazine built in 1831, and the Memorial, which was unveiled by Queen Elizabeth II in 1964, are both interesting sites. The Memorial is dedicated to the memory of the soldiers of the Royal 22nd Regiment killed in service. It was conceived by Georges Vanier, former Governor-General of Canada, and was put up on the occasion of the fiftieth anniversary of the founding of the Regiment in 1964.

A Celebrated Escape

Construction of the Citadel was barely finished when the celebrated escape of the Americans Theller and Dodge occurred. Condemned to be hanged for their part in the Upper-Canada Rebellion of 1837, the Americans had been granted a stay of execution because the Canadian Irish community had alleged that the prisoners could not be found guilty of treason against the English crown because they were Americans. From Toronto, they had been brought to Québec before being sent to England.

During the night of October 15-16, 1838, the day before their departure for London, they were sucessful in escaping from the Citadel along with their prison-mates. The complicity of Québec citizens, among whom were Charles Drolet, lawyer and deputy for Saguenay, John Heath and Édouard Brousseau, permitted Dodge and Theller, (who were luckier than their co-escapees), to reach the American border.

Napoléon Aubin, a journalist with *Fantasque*, took advantage of the event to poke fun at the public administration. Rejecting the facts of the case which were that the prisoners had managed to intoxicate the guards, Aubin explained the Americans' escape this way: "Mr Wakefield (government advisor and amateur hypnotist) visited the captivies and initiated them into the mysteries of 'cogliostroism', that is, hypnotism." He further wrote, "The prisoners put Mr. Wakefield's lessons into practice and simply hypnotized the sentries". In the same mocking tone, Aubin finished the article by teasing the police force whose searches had come to nothing. "We know that Dodge had only one eye, having lost the other in the Revolt. All the one-eyed men in town were therefore rounded up and brought to the police station in hand cuffs. There they were paraded and surrounded by soldiers and policemen, then released after several hours in prison.

Maison Sewell

Maison Sewel, located at 87 Saint-Louis, is an excellent example of English Palladian architecture of the early nineteeth century which is characterized by the presence of pediments, large window and a generally sober and monumental feeling. This house belonged to Judge Jonathan Sewell who lived there for thirty years and raised twenty-two children.

Sewell had fled the United States for England at the out break of the American Revolution and later established himself in Canada where he occupied a number of important public positions. In 1793, he was the solicitor-general and inspector of Crown lands. In 1795, he became the Attorney-General and the following year he became judge of the court of the Vice-Admiralty. Deputy for William-Henry and member of both the legislature and executive councils, he was later named chief justice. At a time when the rights of Francophones were not yet insured Judge Sewell was one of the fiercest adversaries of the French community. He spared nothing in his efforts to anglicize the Francophone population and to abolish the Catholic parishes. He was one of the supporters of the Royal Institution which was devoted to the anglicization of Francophones.

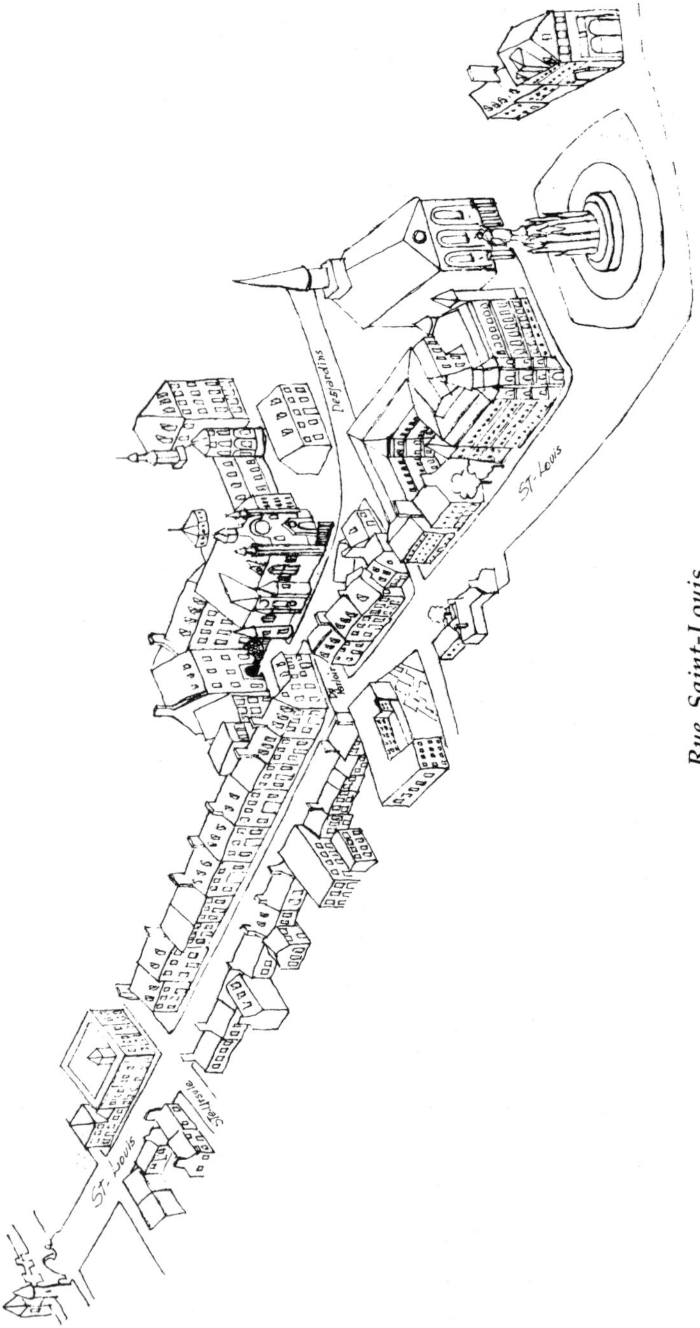

Rue Saint-Louis

Things were to change rapidly. After the Act of Union in 1841 and, above all, at the time of Confederation, the Anglophones needed Francophone support to form a stable government and to have the proposed confederation accepted. Certain compromises had to be made. Thus it was that one of Judge Sewell's sons became, they say, dean of the faculty of medicine at the very Catholic Université Laval of Québec City.

The Garrison Club

The Garrison Club, next door to the maison Sewell was founded in 1879 by Lieutenant-Colonel Duchesneau and is the oldest military club in Canada. Originally reserved for officers, civilian men were later admitted and, in recent years, women have gained the same right. The club is now amalgamated with the "Circle Universitaire" located at 65 D'Auteuil.

Maison Cureux

Maison Cureux is located at 86 rue Saint-Louis. The house was built in 1729 and classified as an historical monument in 1965. The old sloping roof with dormer-windows was replaced around 1890 by the present mansard roof. At the beginning of the colony, the use of the mansard roof with its wooden framework was quickly stopped because of the fire hazard it posed. It came back into style at the end of the 19th century.

The "General's House"

The house at 72 rue Saint-Louis was built on the site of the house where the mortal remains of the American general, Richard Montgomery, were taken. The latter was killed at the bottom of Cap Diamant, near Place Royale, during the siege of Québec on December 31, 1775. On January 4, 1776, the body of the defeated general was buried near the powder magazine of the Saint-Louis bastion. The general's body had been identified by a Mr. Thompson and by Mrs. Prentice, with whom Montgomery, when he was a captain in Wolfe's army, had stayed after the Conquest. In 1818, the body of Montgomery was unearthed and returned to the United States at the request of the general's widow.

Maison Péan

Maison Péan, at 59 rue Saint-Louis, was built around 1750. It was inhabited by Michel-Jean-Hugues Péan of whom "all the good qualities," wrote mockingly the anonymous author of *Mémoire du Canada*, "consisted of the charms of his wife", Angélique Renaud d'Avène de Méloizes. Born in Québec in 1722, this woman, who had gone to the Ursuline boarding school in Québec, was at the centre of numerous love affairs, embellished or deformed by legend, involving many important personnages of New France, including Intendant Bigot.

Michel Péan, a favourite of Bigot, amassed an immense fortune. After the Conquest, he was involved in "the Canada Affair". The French authorities were dismayed by the loss of New France; they needed a scapegoat. With the Ministers of the Navy and War beyond reproach, with Montcalm dead, and with the King's refusal to allow His Majesty's battalions to be blamed, only the government of New France was left.

First of all, the Marquis de Vaudreuil was criticized for having signed the capitulation of Montréal too quickly without being granted the honours of war. However, he had thus acted in order to save the lives of many Canadians and the useless destruction of much property. According to Lévis, the marquis "had done everything humanly possible up to the very last moment."[16] Vaudreuil was exonerated.

As for François Bigot and his accomplices, who had profited from the war and the political situation to accumulate huge fortunes, they received heavy sentences. Bigot lost all his possessions, paid heavy fines, and was banished from the Kingdom of France for life. He lived in exile in Switzerland thanks, supposedly, to the generosity of his former friends. The Péans were permitted to live in France where they settled in Touraine. Following the death of her husband in 1782, Angélique de Méloizes dedicated her final years to the service of the under privileged and the Canadian families living in the area. She died on December 1, 1792.

An Historic Cannonball

Between 59 and 55½ rue Saint-Louis, you will find a cannonball trapped in the roots of a tree. It is said to date from the War of 1759 when it was "planted"; it "grew" with the tree.

Joseph Bouchette

Joseph Bouchette, horseman, Surveyor General of Lower Canada, and Lieutenant-Colonel of the Canadian Militia, lived at 44 rue Saint-Louis. He was the author of several important scientific works including a Topographical Description of the Province of Lower Canada published in 1815. He also drew up the border between Canada and the United States, in accordance with the Treaty of Ghent of 1814. This line was later redrawn, and with the Treaty of Ashburton in 1842, the border between the State of Maine and the Province of Québec was set further North.

Joseph Bouchette was an important man, and the fact that his father had once saved Carleton, the governor of the colony, from the American invaders probably contributed to his being in the favour of the colonial authorities. It is to be remembered that at the time of the American Revolution, Carleton barely escaped from the Americans, who were about to take Montréal. He arrived by canoe at Québec disguised as a "habitant". Joseph Bouchette's father was the leader of the expedition.

An Important Detour: The Ursuline Convent

The Ursuline Convent is located on rue du Parloir. The Ursulines arrived in New France in 1639 at the same time as the Hospitalières, founders of the Hôtel-Dieu Hospital of Québec. The Ursulines, devoted to teaching young French and Amerindian girls, first settled in a house in the Lower Town. Afterwards, they built their convent in the Upper Town, under the able leadership of Marie de l'Incarnation and thanks to the financial help of their benefactoress, Madame de la Peltrie. The building, destroyed by fire in 1650, was rebuilt the following year. The first church, founded in 1658, burned down in 1720. The present church dates back to 1901. An altar-piece, the work of Pierre-Noël Levasseur, executed around 1730, was placed in the new place of worship. The Monument Marie de l'Incarnation, across from the building, is the work of the sculptor Émile Brunet. It was decided to built the monument in 1939, on the occasion of the three hundredth anniversary of the arrival in New France of Marie de l'Incarnation who, by her courage, her tenacity and saintliness, was one of the leading figures of New France. It is said that the local authorities consulted her even about financial questions. The many writings that she left are of inestimable historical value.

The Ursulines Museum, at 12 rue Donnacona, is open to visitors. It was set up in a house built in 1836, which, according to the building contract, was made with the foundation, the old stones, and the old wood of the house which had belonged to the aforementioned Madame de la Peltrie. It was erected in 1644 and enlarged four years later. The house served as a residence for the Ursulines, for Mgr de Laval, and for the "filles du Roy", young ladies sent to New France to find husbands; it was also used as teacher's college. The Ursuline Museum preserves many collector's items. Some, like General Montcalm's skull, are quite peculiar; others, saved from the 1686 fire, are very old. They are a reminder of the important role played by the community from the start of the colony up until today. The institution has always enjoyed an excellent reputation. Governors Dorchester and Prescott sent their daughters there to learn to speak French.

At the corner of Des Jardins and Donnacona is said to stand the building with the narrowest facade in North America. Rue Donnacona was named in honour of an Amerindian chief that Cartier took back to France after his second voyage to America in 1536. Cartier, by taking Donnacona away, wanted to facilitate the rise of a rival chief, Agona, to the head of the large village of Stadacona (Québec City). In 1541, out of the nine Amerindians taken to

The Ursuline Chapel and Museum

Compagnie franche de la Marine face à Notre-Dame des Victoires. *(Photo J. Boutet)*

Le 22e Régim
à l'hôtel de ville.
(Photo J. Boutet)

Bse Marie de l'Incarnation (1599-1672)

France at the same time as Donnacona, only a young ten-year-old girl remained and there was no question of bringing her back to America. Cartier, upon his return to Québec, explained to the inhabitants of Stadacona, who were suprised at not seeing their friends again, that the latter had preferred the comforts of France to their homeland.

Maison Jacquet

Maison Jacquet, at the corner of Saint-Louis and Des Jardins, is made up of two buildings. The one set back from the street on the corner, which dates back to 1677, is probably one of the oldest buildings in Québec City. The other, along with the extension on rue Des Jardins, was built in the 19 th century on the site of the stable and the inner courtyard designed by Pierre Menage in the 16th century.

Maison Vanfelson, located at 13, 15, and 17 rue Des Jardins, still has its stone stables built around 1780.

Maison Jacquet was called Montcalm House for a long time because of the unfounded belief that Montcalm had died there in 1759. The writer Philippe Aubert de Gaspé owned the house and lived in it from 1815 to 1824.

The Duke of Kent's House

Opposite Maison Jacquet, at 25 rue Saint-Louis, is one of the oldest, if not the oldest, house in Québec City. Built around 1650, at the request of Louis D'Ailleboust, Governor of New France, the building has undergone several tranformations. When the governor died, his widow, Marie Barbe de Boulogne continued to live in it until 1670, when she sold it to the Hospitallières of Hôtel-Dieu Hospital, with whom she went to live.

The Duke of Kent, Queen Victoria's father, who arrived in Québec City in August 1791, lived in the house for three years. These were, it is said, the best years of his life; they were spent there with the beautiful Madame de Saint-Laurent. In 1818, the Duke of Kent, after a twenty-eight-year love affair, had to leave the beautiful lady to marry a princess of royal blood. Queen Victoria was born of this marriage. As for Madame de Saint-Laurent, it is said she retired to a convent in Smyrne.

It was in this house in 1759 that M. de Ramezay signed the capitulation of Québec in the absence of Governor Vaudreuil who had stayed with the army.

Jean-Baptiste-Nicolas-Roch de Ramezay was the son of the governor of Montréal. In Québec, he was responsible for the defence of the Upper Town. Hospitalized during the summer, he took back the command of his men on September 13, 1759, upon learning of Montcalm's defeat. The same evening, Vaudreuil sent him the terms of surrender which had been approved by Montcalm, along with an order warning him "not to wait for the enemy to carry the day in battle. Thus, as soon as the food supplies gave out, he would raise the white flag." On September 15, the bourgeois of Québec recommended that Ramezay surrender. At a war council, 13 out of 14 officers approved the request. Meanwhile, the defence of the colony was being organized. Vaudreuil met Lévis, back from Montréal, a few kilometres from Québec. On September 17, the governor had a letter delivered to Ramezay ordering him to resist. But it was too late; Ramezay had made his decision. On the 18th, Charles Saunders and George Townshend signed the articles of surrender in the name of England. To have resisted for a short time might have forced the English to raise the siege and leave in order to avoid an early winter or being defeated by a French counter-offensive.

The number of sick and wounded, the pressure exerted by the bourgeois, the desertion of a large number of officers, and the threat of a landing probably led Ramezay to make this decision, thus giving the English armies a strategic position. All this was contained in Townshend's report to the king.

Maison Maillou

Maison Maillou is located at 17 rue Saint-Louis, just before you reach Place d'Armes. Built without a second floor around 1736 by Jean Maillou, the house was raised to its present height before the end of the French Régime. If you look carefully, you can see the line which separates the two floors. In 1799, John Hale had a vault built with walls two metres (6 feet) thick, which it is said, protected up to 100 000 pounds sterling of the English royal treasury.

Back at Place d'Armes

From Maison Maillou, you go back down rue Saint-Louis to Place d'Armes. If you were one of the rich travellers visiting Québec during the last century, you would probably head towards the Hôtel-Union, at 12 rue Sainte-Anne. Built in 1805 at the request of the bourgeois of Québec, the hotel was, at that time, of "the utmost respectability". In spite of its choice site, across from the Governors' Resi-

dence and close to the government buildings, the establisment was not the financial success that it was hoped it would be. It had many owners and fulfilled many functions. The building housed the Executive Council while the Parliament was being constructed, and, in 1884, a tailor named David Morgan lived there. Between 1820 and 1851, the hotel was used many a time as a concert hall and a ballroom. The bourgeois of Québec met there to prepare their request for the incorporation of the city, which was granted by the authorities in 1833. The building also housed the Literary and Historical Society and, later, the workshop for the *Journal de Québec*. Purchased in 1960 by the Québec Government, the building now houses the provincial tourist bureau. The abundant documentation found there provides enough information to plan more than one trip around the Province of Québec.

The Tour of Greater Québec

Following the example of Arthur Buies, nineteenth-century journalist and chronicler, we now invite you to make the tour of Greater Québec. Discover "Charlesbourg with its dazzling white rustic homes; or Beauport, which stretches out for about two leagues and presents an uninterrupted vista of charming villas and peaceful green fields, all coming to an abrupt end at the deep abyss of Montmorency Falls...."[1]

The itinerary is precise and allows visitors to take in the main tourist attractions of the Québec City area. The commentary is indicative rather than descriptive in keeping with a more traditional tour of the region. The excursion, including visits to Cap-Tourmente and Île d'Orléans (Orleans Island) is about 200 kilometres (160 miles) in length. The itinerary can easily be modified or shortened. The starting point is in front of the Assemblée Nationale Building on Avenue Dufferin.

Toward the Hôpital Général Convent

00 km. (0 miles) — **Departure from Government House. Follow Avenue Dufferin to the Grande Allée East.**

0.1 km. (0.06 miles) — **Turn right onto the Grande Allée.**

1.2 km. (0.74 miles) — **Turn right onto Avenue Salaberry.**

St. Patrick's Irish Catholic Church, at the corner of the Grande Allée an Avenue Salaberry, and the Krieghoff House, located at 115 Grande Allée, are noteworthy. The painter Krieghoff was born in Amsterdam in 1815. He came to North America where he first stayed in the United States. Following his marriage to a French-Canadian woman in 1839, he and his wife moved to Montréal, then to Toronto, New York, and, finally, Québec City. Krieghoff rented the house on the Grande Allée at the end of the 1850's. He was greatly inspired by the rural community and the beauty of the region surrounding Québec.

1.7 km. (1.05 miles) — **Note the Jewish Synagogue at the corner of Avenue Salaberry and rue Crémazie.**

2.0 km. (1.24 miles) — **Take in the view of the Lower Town from the top of the Côte Salaberry (Salaberry Hill). The Lower Town was where naval construction workers and the workers in the shoemaking industry set up residence in another era.**

2.2 km. (1.36 miles)	On your left, you will see the windmill built by the nuns of the Hôpital Général in 1709.
2.8 km. (1.73 miles)	Stop. The Convent and Hôpital Général of Québec.

The Convent and Hôpital Général de Québec, 260 Boulevard Langelier

The Hôpital Général was founded in 1692 by Mgr. de Saint-Vallier and is one of the oldest buildings in Québec City. Because it is located outside the walls of the old city, it was spared the shelling of the different sièges. At the time of the Conquest, the nuns from the Hotel-Dieu and from the Ursuline Convent sought refuge at the hospital. The institution took care of all the wounded, making no distinction between the French and British soldiers. The hospital was not touched by the fire which destroyed much of the Lower Town in 1866 — a miracle, some would say. The chapel of the Convent was recently restored. It and the museum make for interesting visits. The latter contains many objects dating from the French Régime, including several once belonging to Mgr. de Saint-Vallier, the hospital's benefactor. The Hôpital Général still fills its original role of taking care of elderly people. A visit to the former Récollet chapel and the museum is by appointment only. For reservations, call 529-0931, extension 228.

From the Hôpital Général to parc Cartier-Brébeuf

00 km. (00 miles)	On leaving the hospital parking lot, turn left onto rue des Commissaire est.
0.1 km. (.06 miles)	Turn left onto rue Saint-Anselme.
0.5 km. (.31 miles)	Keep to the left. Go by the Rock City Tobacco Company.
0.8 km. (.49 miles)	Take 4e Rue, Pont Drouin (Drouin Bridge).
1.2 km. (.74 miles)	Turn left onto 1re Avenue.
1.8 km. (1.12 miles)	Turn left onto Avenue Jacques-Cartier.
2.1 km. (1.3 miles)	Straight ahead on rue Cadillac.
2.3 km. (1.43 miles)	Turn left onto rue de l'Espinay.
2.4 km. (1.49 miles)	Stop at parc Cartier-Brébeuf, 175 rue de l'Espinay.

Parc Cartier-Brébeuf

Visiting hours from April to the end of September are from 9 a.m. (1 p.m. on Mondays) to 5 p.m., and for the rest of the year, Tuesday to Friday from 9 a.m. to 4:30 p.m.. Telephone: 694-4038.

This area was the site of two important historical events. First, Jacques Cartier made his winter camp here during his second voyage to America in 1535. Second, it was here that the first Jesuit missionaries arrived in 1625. Among them was Father Jean de Brébeuf, later martyred in Huronia. The Jesuits built one of their first missions in New France on this site (other missions had been built earlier in Acadia).

A 24 metre long reproduction of Cartier's ship, Grande Hermine, is the park's centre of attraction. She was built in Montréal in 1966 with 16th century tools and techniques. She was on display at the Montréal World's Fair in 1967 (Expo 67) before being moved to parc Cartier-Brébeuf. A metal cross 8 metres high was put up in 1935 to symbolize the cross planted by Cartier in 1535. There is also a granite monument honouring the memory of Father de Brébeuf, Jesuit martyr.

From parc Cartier-Brébeuf to the "Trait-Carré" of Charlesbourg

00 km. (00 miles)	From parc Cartier-Brébeuf, turn right onto de l'Espinay.
0.1 km. (.06 miles)	Turn right onto rue Cadillac.
0.2 km. (.12 miles)	Turn left to rue Royal-Rossilon.
0.3 km. (.18 miles)	Note the outside staircases of the houses to your right on rue Aiguebelle and Avenue La Sarre. They are typical of the Limoilou district of the city.
0.5 km. (.31 miles)	Turn left onto 1re Avenue.
4.0 km. (2.48 miles)	On your left, you will see the maison Eudiste.
4.1 km. (2.54 miles)	Keep left.
5.5 km. (3.42 miles)	Saint-Charles-Borromée Church on 1er Avenue at the corner of 80e Street East.

Saint-Charles-Borromée Church (1825) and the presbytery (1875) are two imposing buildings. The old houses of the area, including the Pierre Lefevre House (1846), 7985 Trait-Carré est, and the former Jesuit communal mill (1733-1744) across from 215, 80th Street East, are also of interest.

The town plans of Charlesbourg and neighbouring Bourg-Royal to the east were drawn up by Jean Talon. Instead of the traditional system of rows, the Intendant used a star-shaped pattern. The streets of Charlesbourg have kept their original layout. They radiate from the central point, the Trait-Carré. The triangular tracts of land surrounding the church made it easy for the inhabitants to seek refuge in the church in case of attack.

The Québec Zoological Gardens are located in Orsainville, a few kilometres north of Charlesbourg. They are worth a visit. The zoo is built on a site where there were once several mills. The Departments of History, Geography, and Civilization of Collège François-Xavier Garneau has undertaken archeological digs on the site.

From the Trait-Carré to Chutes Montmorency

00 km. (00 miles)	From Saint-Charles-Borromée Church, follow 80e Rue Est.
0.2 km. (.12 miles)	Turn right onto Boulevard Henri-Bourassa.
1.2 km. (.74 miles)	Keep to the left.
5.3 km. (3.29 miles)	Turn left onto Chemin de la Canardière (Highway 138).
5.5 km. (3.42 miles)	Turn right onto Avenue de Vitré.
6.3 km. (3.91 miles)	Turn left onto Boulevard Montmorency
6.8 km. (4.22 miles)	Stop at the Maizerets Estate.

The entrance to the Maizerets Estate is immediately to your right. The first building was built in 1705 but burned down by the Americans during the siege of 1776. It was immediately rebuilt in 1777. Two extensions were added on in 1826 and 1849. The estate was the property of the Seminaire de Québec for a long time. In fact, it was named after Louis Ango de Maizerets, the Séminaire's superior in 1705. The domain is now the property of the city of Québec.

6.8 km. (4.22 miles)	On leaving the Maizerets Estate, turn right onto Boulevard Montmorency (heading east).
7.7 km. (4.78 miles)	Turn left onto rue D'Estimauville.
8.1 km. (5.03 miles)	Turn right onto de la Canardière (Route 360 East).
8.2 km. (5.09 miles)	De la Canardière becomes Chemin Royal. You are entering the Beauport city limits. Beauport was founded in 1634 by Robert Gif-

	fard, the first doctor at the Hôtel-Dieu Hospital. It was the first parish on the Beaupré coast. There are many old residences in the city.
10.2 km. (6.34 miles)	A plaque at 488 Avenue Royale indicates the birthplace of Charles-Michel de Salaberry, who defeated the Americans at Châteauguay in 1813. The present building, Manoir Salaberry, was built on the site of the former house.
10.7 km. (6.65 miles)	Note Maison Girardin, across from the row of houses on rue du Couvent. Note also the "saw tooth" arrangement of the houses on Avenue Royale.
15.3 km. (9.51 miles)	Stop at Manoir Montmorency located at 2490 Avenue Royale. From this site, there is a magnificent view of the Chutes Montmorency.

Chute Montmorency (Montmorency Falls)

Chute Montmorency was probably named by Champlain in honour of Admiral Charles de Montmorency, Duke d'Ampville, in 1603. The Falls are 84 metres high, which means 30 metres higher than Niagara Falls. In the winter, when the spray of the falls freezes, a picturesque ice-mountain, called the "pain de sucre" ("Sugarloaf") is formed. Observation platforms have been built at the top and to the south of the falls.

The manoir Montmorency, situated at the top of the falls, is owned by the Government of Québec. It was built in 1781 by Haldimand, Governor-General of Canada from 1778 to 1785. The Duke of Kent, Queen Victoria's father, lived there during his visit to Québec City from 1791 to 1794.

Four bridges have been built at the top of the falls — the first one in 1839. The second, finished in 1856, collapsed several months after its completion, causing the death of three people. The building of the third one was started in 1857, and that of the present bridge in 1923.

The rivière Montmorency separated the French and English armies at the time of the Conquest.

From Chute Montmorency to the Île D'Orléans

00 km. (00 miles)	Leaving the manoir Montmorency parking lot, turn right onto Avenue Royale.
0.6 km. (.37 miles)	Stop at parc Montmorency.
0.6 km. (.7 miles)	Leaving parc Montmorency, turn right onto Avenue Royale.
1.6 km. (.99 miles)	Turn right onto Côte de l'Église.
2.4 km. (1.49 miles)	Turn right onto autoroute Montmorency (Montmorency Highway).
3.5 km. (2.17 miles)	Stop at parc Montmorency at the bottom of the falls.
3.5 km. (2.17 miles)	Leaving parc Montmorency, turn right onto autoroute Montmorency (Montmorency Highway).
4.2 km. (2.61 miles)	Exit for the Île d'Orléans. The road that goes around the island is 67 km. (41.6 miles) long.

Île d'Orléans

The "Île" or island, is 34 km (21 miles) long, and its maximum width is about 9 km (5 miles). Jacques Cartier named it Bacchus, because of the wild grapes that grew there. He then gave it the name "d'Orléans" in honour of the Duke d'Orléans, son of François I. People called it "Witch's Island" for a long time. In the evening, the will-o-the-wisps appeared.

In 1642, the island was offered to Maisonneuve. The latter refused Governor Montmagny's offer, preferring to settle in Ville-Marie (Montréal). The first settlements date back to 1648. The island now has six parishes whose churches and old houses are of great interest. From the village of Sainte-Pétronille at the western tip of the island, the view of Québec is magnificent. Wolfe set up an entrenched camp there in 1759 from where he could watch the movements of the French army. The Hurons who survived Iroquois attacks settled there in the mid-17th century. A shipbuilding industry was established and the two biggest wooden ships ever built in Canada, the *Columbus* (1824) and the *Baron Renfrew* (1825) were launched from there. The manoir Mauvide-Genest, in Saint-Jean, dates back to 1734. The Germans tried to set up installations for spying purposes at Saint-François, at the eastern end of the island. The Canadian military authorities quickly stepped in to stop their activities. The church at Sainte-Famille (1734) is one of the most beautiful on the island. Near Saint-Pierre, the view of the north shore and of the chute Montmorency is magnificent. A bridge has linked the island to the mainland since 1935. The saltwater stops at Île d'Orléans. People used to say that since the salty air was so close, the pasturelands were of better quality. If only the island could talk, the stories it would have to tell — the arrival of Marie de l'Incarnation in 1639, the coming of the Congregation Nuns in 1685, the death of Jean Lauzon, maréchal of New France, the Anne Emard trial at the end of the 17th century....

East from Île d'Orléans

At the Île d'Orléans bridge exit, take highway 40 est, toward Sainte-Anne de Beaupré.

The highway takes you to the Sanctuary of Sainte-Anne de Beaupré, to parc Mont Sainte-Anne, and to the National Wildlife Reserve at Cap Tourmente. The return trip is approximately seventy kilometres long.

Sainte-Anne de Beaupré

A sanctuary dedicated to Sainte-Anne has attracted thousands of pilgrims for several centuries. In 1665, Marie de l'Incarnation wrote to her son, "Seven leagues from here is Sainte-Anne Church, where the paralytic walk, the blind see, and the sick, whatever their illness, are healed." When the first church was being built, in 1658, a worker was healed thanks to the intercession of the good Sainte-Anne, and since then many miracles have been reported. Navigators used to fire a cannon shot to hail their patron saint as they sailed past the church.

Each year, more than a million pilgrims visit the sanctuary, the neo-Roman basilica (1932), the Historial, the wax museum which illustrates the sanctuary's history, the art gallery, and the Cyclorama, a panorama painted in 1882 depicting Jerusalem and the Holy Land at the time of Christ. Out of this number, 13% come from the United States, 80% from the Province of Québec, and 7% from the other Canadian provinces and from Europe. Many Gypsies and Amerindians meet there on Sainte Anne's Day, July 26. Of more than 200 000 copies of the magazine *Sainte-Anne de Beaupré*, published by the sanctuary administered by the Redemptorists, 70 000 are printed in English.

Parc Mont Saint-Anne (access indicated at Beaupré)

A few kilometres east of Sainte-Anne de Beaupré is located parc Mont Sainte-Anne with its numerous Alpine ski

slopes and cross-country ski trails, the park is one of the largest winter sports centres in Canada. Here a great many national as well as international ski competitions alpine, ski jumping and cross-country are held. The park is open all year round. In the summer, sports enthusiasts play golf, cycle or hike. An excursion to the chutes Larose, 68 metres high, is possible.

The National Wildlife Reserve at Cap Tourmente (access indicated at Beaupré).

The national nature reserve at Cap Tourmente, administered by the Canada Wildlife Service, is located east of Saint-Joachim. Guided tours and the viewing of films are organized from May to October, from 10 a.m. to 6 p.m.. A path leads to a cliff where visitors can admire the some 100 000 Snow geese which gather on the coast of the Saint-Laurent, fall and şpring, for their great migration.

An information centre has been set up in the Petite Ferme (Small Farm) which once was the manor of Monseigneur François de Laval, the first bishop of Québec (1674-1684).

The building is found on the site of a farm which Samuel de Champlain had built: "I decided then to build as quickly as possible; although it was July, I nevertheless employed most of the workmen to build this lodging the stable 60 feet long and 20 feet wide, and two other dwellings, each 18 feet by 15 freet, made of wood and earth like those which are built in the villages of Normandy."[2]

West from Île d'Orléans

00 km. (00 miles)	On leaving the island, take Highway 40 west (ouest) toward Québec.
1.7 km. (1.05 miles)	Take the exit indicating Highway 440 Ouest toward Québec. As you drive along, a magnificent panorama of the city unfolds before your eyes.
8.6 km. (5.34 miles)	Take Exit 23 (sortie 23) — Boulevard Henri-Bourassa.
12.4 km. (7.7 miles)	Take the highway 40 ouest Exit toward Montréal.
18.0 km. (11.2 miles)	Take Boulevard Saint-Jacques (Exit 310). Arnaud and Rue Celles lead to Boulevard Saint-Jacques.
20.7 km. (12.8 miles)	Turn right onto Boulevard Saint-Jacques.

25.0 km. (15.5 miles)	Turn left onto Route 369 nord.
25.7 km. (15.9 miles)	The limits of the Village Huron.
26.0 km. (16.2 miles)	Notre-Dame-de-Lorette Church.

The Village Huron

With the arrival of the first French-Canadian settlers in Ancienne-Lorette in 1697, the Hurons were forced to look for a new place to live, even though they had been at the previous site since 1673. They went north and finally settled along the rivière Saint-Charles near the chutes Kabir Koubat, Notre-Dame-de-Lorette Chapel was built in 1730. In 1862, it was partially destroyed by fire, but immediately rebuilt according to the original model. It contains many very old works of art, including a silver lamp made by François Ranvoyzé (1739-1819).

From the Village Huron to the Vieille Maison des Jésuites

00 km. (00 miles)	From rue Rivière du Serpent (Snake River Street), turn right onto Route 369 nord.
0.1 km. (.06 miles)	Straight through the traffic lights at des Étudiants Boulevard.
0.7 km. (.43 miles)	Turn left onto Boulevard Valcartier.
1.1 km. (.68 miles)	Turn right onto rue Racine.
1.9 km. (1.18 miles)	Keep to the left at the top of the hill.
2.3 km. (1.42 miles)	Turn left onto Route 371 sud.
6.9 km. (4.28 miles)	Take Highway 40 ouest in the direction of the pont Pierre-Laporte.
8.2 km. (5.09 miles)	Continue toward the pont Pierre-Laporte.
12.0 km. (7.45 miles)	Take Boulevard Charest ouest (Highway 440 West).
14.4 km. (8.94 miles)	Take Highway 540 South toward the pont Pierre-Laporte.
18.7 km. (11.6 miles)	Continue on Highway 540 Sud toward the pont Pierre-Laporte. The pont de Québec, built in 1917 is the longest cantilevered bridge in the world, and the pont Pierre-Laporte, opened in 1970, is the longest suspension bridge in Canada.

20.2 km. (12.5 miles)	Take the Boulevard Champlain Exit (Sortie 132).
20.5 km. (12.7 miles)	Turn left onto Boulevard Champlain.
25.0 km. (15.5 miles)	Turn left and follow the signs to the old La vieille maison des Jésuites (Jesuit House).
26.0 km. (16.2 miles)	Stop at the Vieille Maison des Jésuites.

The Vieille Maison des Jésuites

The Jesuits arrived in New France in 1625 and set up a mission on this site in 1637. Noël Brulart de Sillery, a member of the Knights of Malta and of the Compagnie des Cents-Associés, provided the financial backing for the founding of the mission. The city of Sillery was named to honour the memory of this illustrious benefactor. The first house built in the same year as the mission was destroyed by fire in 1657. It was rebuilt in 1660. The Jesuits abandoned the mission in 1698, and, after that date, the house had a number of different owners. Mrs. Brooke, the English author of the first novel written and set in Canada (*The History of Émilie Montague*), lived there. Near the house, there is a monument dedicated to Father Ennemond Massé, the mission's superior, and to Commander Brûlart de Sillery. The monument is a reminder of the first church built for the Amerindians in New France. It was built in 1644 and demolished in 1824. At the intersection leading to Boulevard Champlain, there is a plaque pointing out the site of the first Hôtel-Dieu Hospital in America. Construction was begun in 1640. Four years later, the Hospitalière Nuns found that the site was not secure enough and too far from the settlement; they moved the hospital to the top of Côte du Palais.

The Maison des Jésuites is open to visitors from 9 a.m. to 5 p.m. during the summer. The museum collection includes Amerindian objects, historical documents, and manuscripts dealing with the history of the Jesuits.
(Telephone: 653-4776)

Back to the Legislative Complex

From Chemin du Foulon, take Boulevard Champlain est as far as Côte Gilmour, which was once used by the armies of Wolfe and Montgomery. This road takes you to the Plains of Abraham. If you continue in an easterly direction, you will return to your starting point.

You can also take the following:

00 km. (00 miles)	On leaving the Vieille Maison des Jésuites, head east on Chemin du Foulon.
0.9 km. (.55 miles)	Turn left onto Côte de l'Église (Church Hill).
1.5 km (.93 miles)	Stop at Saint-Michel (formerly, Saint-Colomban) Church. The Church was built between 1852 and 1854 according to the plans of the architect Goodlate Richardson Browne. From the church's parking lot, there is a splendid view of the river. Other vantage points are accessible if you take Avenue des Voiliers, a few metres from the church.
1.5 km. (.93 miles)	Turn left on leaving the church's parking lot.
2.3 km. (1.43 miles)	Turn left onto Chemin Saint-Louis (Saint-Louis Road).
3.4 km. (2.11 miles)	Keep right.
5.8 km. (3.6 miles)	The Assemblée Nationale Building. End of the excursion.

Québec City and the North American continent

The Days of Stadacona

The city of Québec has long been a centre of North American commercial exchange. Well before the arrival of the Europeans, Stadacona (Quebec City) was an important centre of commerce. According to geographer Raoul Blanchard, the Amerindians of what is now the United States travelled up the Kennebec and Chaudière Rivers to exchange their agricultural products for furs.

At that time, the principal Amerindian nations were spread over an area which encompasses both sides of the present Canadian-American border. The territory of the Abenakis, Etchemins, and Micmacs extended south of the present border and that of the Iroquois was, to a large extent, within the United States. Exchanges between these tribes were numerous. The fleuve Saint-Laurent and its tributaries invited commerce. The Hurons and Iroquois, who lived between the rivière Richelieu and the Great Lakes, produced corn, tobacco, and animal snares. The Indians of the golfe du Saint-Laurent offered fish, smoked meat, and moose hide, while those on the south shore had furs for trade. The smaller tribes of the Atlantic coast offered mostly wampum, a sort of bracelet or necklace fashioned from seashells.

Group of Hurons
(From a painting by Georges Heriot, 1807)

The arrival of the first Europeans effectively put an end to these exchanges. Within a very few years the commercial trade network established by the Amerindians was completely transformed to the benefit of the new arrivals.

The Europeans in America

The seizure of Constantinople by the Turks in 1453 severely damaged trade between Europe and Asia and drove the Europeans to search for new routes to Asia. New financial resources resulting from the Crusades as well as new seafaring techniques — such as the use of the compass and the stern post rudder — and a greatly expanded knowledge of cosmography (the science of describing the world), facilitated the organization of new expeditions.

The Portuguese were the first to take up the challenge. Diaz left the Azores in 1432, reached the Cape Verdes Islands in 1446 and, two years later, rounded the tip of Africa and arrived in India. This route, however, was too long to be practical.

The Spanish turned toward the Atlantic. In 1492, Christopher Columbus reached the West Indies which he believed to be just off the coast of Asia. He died in 1506, still firm in his belief that he had been the first to reach the Orient by sailing across the Atlantic.

The rest of Europe was not indifferent to the Spanish and Portuguese discoverers. England joined the movement when, in 1497, Henry VII authorized the departure of the first expedition. The Venetian Giovanni Caboto, better known as John Cabot, set off to conquer the Atlantic. He was searching for north-west passage to Asia. After a voyage of 700 leagues, he reached land. He took possession of this new land in the name of England and then explored the coastline for a distance of 300 leagues. Cabot also made two other voyages to America, one in 1498, and one in 1500.

We have no actual proof of the voyages of Cabot. Traditional history, however, maintains that he reached Newfoundland on his first trip in 1497, and this furthered England's territorial claims at the end of the sixteenth century.

In 1501, the Portuguese sailor Gaspar Corte-Real, and, in 1502, his brother Miguel also reached the Atlantic coast of America. We are unaware of the details of their expeditions except that Gaspar Corte-Real died here and only a part of his fleet returned to Portugal. In 1520, another Portuguese, Joao Alvares Fagundes, tried in vain to establish a colony in southern Newfoundland.

In 1524, France, whose territorial pre-occupations had kept her involved at home, also turned to the Atlantic. Giovanni da Verragano, who was financed by a syndicate in Lyon, set out in search of a route to India. On May 25, 1524, he reached North Carolina near present-day Cape Fear, which he called "Annunciation". The French emissary followed the coastline north as far as Cape Breton without finding a passage west. He baptized the different places he visited. Virginia was called Acadia; the coast of Delaware and New Jersey was Côte-de-Lorraine; Atlantic City was Bonnivet; the Delaware River, Vandôme; New York, Angoulème, and New England was christened "Land of the Evil Race" because of hostile Ameridians whose "barbarity was such that in spite of our signals, we were unable to establish relations."[1]

The Atlantic seaboard was not in French hands for long. Verrazano had barely returned to France when Captain Estevan Gomez seized the territory for Spain and changed the names. After several vain attempts, the Spanish abandoned the area to concentrate their efforts in Florida where they had been established since 1521. The English came next. In 1527, the ships *May Guilford* and *Sampson* reached Cape Breton and followed the coastline south, thus retracing Verrazano's route in reverse. In this way, the English made their first claims to American territory.

The Discovery of Canada by the Europeans

The list of claimants to the discovery of Canada is long. Some accord this honour to Cabot who claimed the coast of Newfoundland for England in 1497. Others claim it was Jacques Cartier who, in the name of the King of France, discovered the fleuve Saint-Laurent, wintered at Stadacona (Québec), and sailed as far as Hochelaga (Montreal) at the end of the 1530's.

Perhaps the credit should go to the Irish. According to the historian Gustave Lanctot, the Irish, hunted by Scandinavian warriors, sought refuge along the coast of Nova Scotia in the 9th century. They were followed two centuries later by the Vikings. Later came Basque, Portuguese, and Breton fishermen; and, finally, in the fifteenth and sixteenth centuries, the English and the French. If we mean, however, by "discoverer of Canada", the first European to realize that the territory was, in fact a continent, then the Breton Jacques Cartier, by his discovery of the Saint-Laurent which he followed as far as Hochelaga (Montreal) in 1535, merits the title.

Anglo-French Rivalry in America

Europeans knew of North America, and men came here to fish for cod long before actually beginning to settle the continent. The English established themselves at Jamestown in 1607, and the French at Québec in 1608. Excluding the Spanish settlements in Georgia and Florida and French attempts in the latter, we can consider Jamestown and Québec as marking the start of the French and English presence in America.

It did not take long for the two empires to come into conflict. They were after the same objectives, including the search for the best fishing and fur territories and the occupation of strategic positions. Along with these reasons, the effects of European conflicts quickly led the colonies to war from Louisiana to Hudson's Bay.

The Amerindians, the first occupants of the land, chose sides. The Hurons, Abenakis, and Montagnais sided with the French, while the Iroquois aligned themselves with the English. Trading posts, which were strategically situated along the various waterways, became fortresses. In 1667, Talon proposed either the purchase or the conquest of New York. The project, later taken up by Callières, was never realized. He wanted to insure better communications between New France and the mother country, as the Saint-Laurent was closed to navigation during the winter months.

The colonies were often at war before hostilities were officially declared. In 1704, a prisoner was taken; she was the maternal ancestor of a future Bishop of Québec, Mgr. Plessis. In 1703, during a raid on the village of Wells, Maine, the Abenakis seized a number of prisoners among whom was Esther Wheelwright, the five-year-old daughter of Captain John Wheelwright. Several years later, Father Bigot was awarded custody of the child and placed her in the care of the Ursuline Sisters of Québec. In 1713, Esther took the veil under the name of Sister Esther Marie-Joseph de l'Enfant-Jesus. On December 15, 1760, Sister Esther, daughter of John Wheelwright, a New England Puritan, former judge in York and counsellor of the Sovereign Council of Boston, was elected Superior of the Ursulines of Québec.

From the founding of the first settlements to the end of the 18th century, there were six major conflicts between the two empires and, each time, Québec was at the centre of the confrontation.

After having successfully resisted the attack of 1627, Champlain, was forced to hand over the city to English emissaries in 1629. France retook the colony three years later. In 1690, Frontenac resisted the assaults by Phips and, in 1711, by Walker, whose fleet had run aground on the reefs at île-aux-Oeufs and was unable to reach Québec. In 1759, during the Seven Years' War, the English finally succeeded in permanently taking the city.

The Jumonville-Washington affair took place in the years immediately preceding this war. Around 1740, the boundaries between the Thirteen Colonies and New France along the Ohio and Mississippi Rivers were rather vague. In order to better ensure their positions, the French built forts and buried lead plaques beneath them. Robert Dinwiddie, Governor of Virginia, believed it neceessary to dislodge the French. He sent a young emissary with a brilliant future, twenty-three-year-old George Washington, to ask the French to leave the territory. The French refused. Dinwiddie then decided to built a fort on the Ohio at the site of present-day Pittsburgh. The French had beaten him to it and were already building Fort Duquesne, named for the Governor of New France.

Dinwiddie decided, therefore, that his best recourse was to arms. "On February 2, 1754, Washington, who had been promoted to lieutenant-colonel, left with a contingent of one hundred and twenty soldiers. On May 27, he arrived at Fort Duquesne. What happened next is not clear. A French detachment, led by Jumonville, was sent to make contact with the English. Perhaps Washington misinterpreted their intentions; in any case, the English opened fire without warning, killing Jumonville and ten of his men. The rest, arguing in vain that no state of war existed between the two countries, were taken prisoner. The French cried murder, while the English called it legitimate self-defence.

Things did not end there. Washington, intoxicated by his success, judged it prudent to cover his retreat. He expected revenge to come further south at the well-named Fort Necessity, but it came sooner. Encircled by Indians allied to the French, the English surrendered after ten hours of fighting.

Here, again, the facts are unclear. Washington knew no French and perhaps was misled by his interpreter, but, for whatever reason, he signed a capitulation to his Most Christian Majesty, the King of France, in which was made mention of the "assassination" of Jumonville.

Disgraced in Canada and France, ridiculed in America and suspect in England, the future president must have believed his military career was finished as he resigned at the end of the year.[2]

Montgomery

Washington was not idle for long. War offered him a chance to regain his reputation. He served under the orders of General Braddock and, as a hero of the War of Independence, became the first President of the United States.

In 1763, the Treaty of Paris put an end to the Seven Years' War, and New France became an English colony. The accord was no sooner signed than discontent again erupted between the old and the new English colonies. The problem of ownership of the territories to the south of the Great Lakes, coveted by both sides during the Seven Years' War, remained unresolved. By ceding the area to Québec, England would have upset the thirteen Colonies and vice versa. It was, therefore, decided to create a "no-man's land" — a solution which pleased no one!

In 1774, England changed its policy and gave the territories in question to Québec. The Thirteen Colonies, already nursing a long list of grievances against England, saw in the Québec Act yet another reason to revolt. The first Continental Congress held in Philadelphia in October of 1774 found the Québec Act intolerable and in the same category as other laws destined to subdue the Thirteen Colonies. War was declared and the taking of Québec once more became the goal of the "Bostoners".

On August 31, 1775, a first army, two thousand strong and led by Schuyler and Montgomery, undertook the invasion of Canada by way of Lake Champlain and the rivière Richelieu. In spite of the resistance of Fort Saint-Jean, the army quickly reached Montréal which capitulated and became until the following spring, an American city. Governor Carleton, disguised as a peasant, just managed to escape to Québec.

At the beginning of December, Montgomery's army joined with that of Benedict Arnold at Québec. Arnold had led his army up from the United States by way of the Kennebec and Chaudière Rivers, the first time that this route had ever been used to invade Canada. The route was considered so treacherous that even during the Amerindian Wars it had not been used. On December 31, 1775, the armies of Arnold and Montgomery, who had vowed to "eat New Year's dinner in Québec or in Hell", attempted their final assault at the height of a blizzard. The contract of many of the mercenaries was to expire the next day. Arnold was wounded in the attack while Montgomery, along with approximately one hundred followers, was killed. The siege lasted until the following spring when the arrival of the English fleet forced the Americans back across their borders. Washington had been right when, in a letter to Shuyler dated January 1776, he wrote "Québec must be taken before spring. If not, the city will be rescued by the arrival of the English fleet."

The retreat of the American armies also obliged the delegates of the Congress who were in Montréal to leave. The American delegation, directed by Benjamin Franklin, Charles Carrol, and Samuel Chase, and assisted by the Jesuit John Carrols, a future Catholic bishop, and the printer Mesplet, had failed in their attempt to incite Montrealers against England. Throughout the conflict, the French-Canadians had preferred neutrality. Against the repeated solicitation of the Americans, they did not budge. Only several hundred Canadians joined the American revolutionary forces. The élite aligned themselves with England. At the end of the winter of 1776, Mgr. Briand announced his intention to refuse the sacrements to the rebels. The Québec Act of 1774, by granting the free exercise of the Catholic faith as well as the use of the French language and French laws, made the choice an easy one for many Francophones.

Fleury Mesplet was the precursor of French journalism in Canada. During the American occupation of Montréal, he printed the Congress's appeals to the inhabitants.

Although defeated at Québec and later at Fort Beausejours, New Brunswick and Niagara, Ontario, the Americans were luckier on their own territory. On October 17, 1777, General Burgoyne, who had forced the Americans from Québec the previous year, was defeated at Saratoga. Two months later, Franklin was officially informed by Vergennes of Frence's decision to intervence on behalf of the United States against England. A treaty of alliance was signed on February 6, 1778, and the revolutionaries predicted an imminent victory.

France's support of their cause made the Americans once more dream of invading Québec. La Fayette, convinced that he could rally the French-Canadians, proposed that Washington launch an invasion of Québec under the auspices of France. Washington refused, perhaps fearful of creating a bothersome neighbour for the future American Republic.

The Treaty of Paris, signed in 1783, officially ended the war. England recognized the independence of the United States, and the new border along the Great Lakes was fixed to the advantage of the Americans. At the signing of the treaty, no mention was made of the money owed by the Americans to the Ursuline Convent at Trois-Rivières. The nuns had nursed the American wounded with the promise of remuneration. That debt, never honored, would today exceed ten million dollars.

Canada Pays the Price of English Diplomacy

England's generosity toward the Unites States did not end with the Treaty of Paris. In order to reconcile the Americans, England did not hesitate to sacrifice large portions of Canadian territory.

The boundaries between Québec, New Brunswick, and the United States were poorly defined after the War of Independence. Despite the Treaty of Ghent (1814), the situation remained unsettled in the 1820's. The arrival of loggers in the area and the threat of an American invasion prompted the parties involved to ask the King of the Netherlands to arbitrate. The proposed solution was rejected by the United States. The Webster-Ashburton Treaty of 1842 finally provided a definitive ruling on the issue to the advantage of the Americans. The Maine border, contrary to first sketches, was advanced much further north.

In 1846, a second agreement between England and the United States fixed the Canadian-American border from the Rocky Mountains to the Pacific on the 49th Parallel, in spite of Canadian rights to territory which extended as far as southern Oregon.

Finally, in 1903, an Anglo-American tribunal defined the boundary between Alaska, which had been acquired from Russia in 1867, and Canada. Once again the decision favoured the United States. Two of the three arbitrators representing England were of Canadian origin and, significantly, disassociated themselves from the majority.

English largesse toward America was not restricted to decisions concerning the border. In 1871, the Treaty of Washington gave the Americans navigational rights on the fleuve Saint-Laurent and the Great Lakes. Canada received reciprocal rights on three rivers in Alaska! In addition, the Americans were given the right to fish in Canadian waters for ten years upon payment of a 500 000$ indemnity. The treaty clearly favoured the United States and John A. Macdonald, the first Canadian Prime Minister, was unable to conceal his unhappiness. Before signing the treaty in the name of England, he looked at the American Secretary of State and said, "Here go the fisheries".

"You have got a good equivalent for them," responded Hamilton Fish.

"No," replied Macdonald, "we give them away." He then signed the treaty and then, as he left the table, added, "They (the fisheries) are gone."[3]

Thanks to effective diplomacy and the Louisiana Purchase of 1803, the United States managed to accrue a large part of New France, of which Québec had been the capital. In the name of the King of France and in the service of the Catholic Church, numerous French explorers had travelled throughout America in search of furs and the best routes for travel.... In 1669, La Salle arrived at Niagara; de Saint-Lusson took possession of the Great Lakes in 1671; Louis Jolliet accompanied by Père Marquette, desended the Mississippi in 1673. In 1682, La Salle took possession of Louisiana. In 1743, the La Verendryes penetrated as far as South Dakota and were the first whites to see the Rockies. A lead plaque, buried in 1743 and discovered near Pierre, South Dakota in 1913, confirms their exploits. More than fifty French forts were constructed on American territory, and many cities were founded by the French of New France. No doubt the most famous of these are Detroit, founded by Lamothe-Cadillac of Montréal in 1701, and St. Louis, named in honour of Louis IX of France and founded by Pierre Laclède in 1764.

The Renewed American Menace

Without a doubt, the benevolent attitude towards the United States was, for England, the best policy to follow. They did not want to lose their North American market, and they felt themselves threatened by the new American power.

In 1812, the United States did not hesitate to declare war and an army of 6 000 invaded Canada. It seemed to some that this would be an easy undertaking. "What a pleasant prospect is open to our volunteers," declared future President Andrew Jackson, the day before the invasion, "to embark on a military excursion to a far-off country." Anglo-Canadian resistance was far stronger than had been imagined. In spite of some victories along the Great Lakes, the Americans were unable to unite their two invading forces. One had come from the west while the other had come north by way of the Richelieu Valley. The Anglo-Canadian victory at Châteauguay prevented the conquest of Canada.

The Treaty of Ghent put an end to this war in 1812, but American hopes of taking possession of Canada were not so easily dashed. Canadians felt more and more treatened. They were worried about the Monroe Doctrine by which any European interference in American affairs was rejected and about the policy of "Manifest Destiny" which led Americans to believe that taking possession of the entire continent was not only in their interest, but their duty, as well. Canadian concern grew with each successive enlargement of American territory: the Louisiana Purchase in 1803, completed in 1819 by a treaty with Spain; the annexation of Texas in 1845, followed by the acquisition of other Mexican territories in 1848; the taking of Canadian land in 1842 and 1849 and the purchase of Alaska in 1867.

Incursions into Canadian territory by the "Fenians," who were devoted to gaining independence for Ireland, added fuel to the fire. During the American Civil War (1860-65), relations between the two countries deteriorated even further. England, officially neutral, could not hide her sympathy for the South, her supplier of cotton.

The capture of the English ship, "Trent", in 1861, on board which were found two English emissaries, and the "Alabama Affair" further damaged relations. (Alabama was a warship built in Liverpool at the request of the Confederate Army.) In return, the Americans spoke of invading Canada which was still an English colony.

The United States — A Threat to be Countered

The fear of an American invasion forced Canada to present a united front to the eventual invaders. Charles de Salaberry, who had beaten back the Americans at Châteauguay in 1813, was recognized as the first "Canadian" hero. Étienne Pascal Taché, an important Québec politician and future Canadian Prime Minister, felt it necessary to declare his loyalty to England. Faced with the American menace he stated that, "the last cannon fired to maintain the English presence in America will be by Canadian hands."

The possibility of war with the United States forced England to re-think the Canadian defence system. The Québec Citadel and the majority of other fortifications in the Québec City region were constructed to protect Canada in the event of an American attack. Fortifications on the south shore were built to insure freedom of movement for the English fleet as well as to prevent the Americans from using the Grand Trunk Railway which had a branch line connecting Lévis and Portland, Maine.

The very fact of Canadian Confederation is due, in large measure, to the American menace. In the event of war with the United States, it would have been important for the inhabitants of the different British-North American colonies to have a railway terminus on the Atlantic. For more than five months of the year, the Saint-Laurent was blocked by ice, and it was impossible to maintain connections with Europe. The only such teminus was at Portland, Maine. The Americans thus held a strategic advantage of great importance. The urgent need for a Canadian railway-port connection on the Atlantic and the desire to counter American expansionism, which was particularly threatening in the West, were the major motivating factors in Canadian Confederation.

In 1867, the first four colonies (Ontario, Québec, New Brunswick and Nova Scotia) formed a federation. Manitoba joined the federation in 1870, followed by British Columbia in 1871, Prince Edward Island in 1873, Saskatchewan and Alberta in 1905, and, finally Newfoundland in 1949. The Yukon and Northwest Territories complete the federation.

In 1867, Canada, following the example of the United States in 1776, drafted a constitution and a judicial system which, in both form and content resembled England's constitutional and judicial law. This fact explains the "analogies between the political structure and actual law of these two North American countries".[4] There exists, however, many fundamental differences between the two constitutions. This is explained, on the one hand, by the evolution of constitutional and judicial law in England between 1776 and 1867, (the modern parliamentary system did not appear until the electoral reforms of the Great Reform Act of 1832) and, on the other hand, by the wish of the Canadian "Fathers of Confederation" to avoid certain American constitutional regulations such as the granting of residuary powers to the states, which was deemed dangerous.

The United States — A Model to Imitate.

If the American constitution was too "liberal" for the "Fathers of Confederation," the American political institutions served as a model for the "Patriots" of 1837-38.

At the end of the 1830's, certain Canadians from Upper Canada (Ontario) and Lower Canada (Quebec), aggravated by England's refusal to grant the majority the right to choose its government and menaced by an economic recession, undertook to make themselves heard by taking up arms. The forces of law and order succeeded in putting down the rebellion in the two provinces. Many of the rebels escaped to the United States. There, the Patriots formed the association known as the Chasseur Brothers which was dedicated to the independence of Lower Canada and whose members were sworn to keep the secrets of the association "under pain of seeing their properties destroyed and having their neck cut to the bone."

The ensuing struggle lasted more than a year. The invasion of Canada by the armies of Upper and Lower Canada failed. In Buffalo, William Lyon Mackenzie, rebel leader of Upper Canada, proclaimed the Republic of Upper Canada. At the same time, Robert Nelson was drafting a declaration of independence which proclaimed the Republic of Lower Canada; this he sent to Canadian newspapers at the end of February, 1838.

Article Two of that declaration would have made Lower Canada a republic after the Americain model. That same idea was to be seized upon again many times by nationalistic Québécois. In 1967, the états généraux du Canada français (a grouping together of the Francophone organizations in Canada) adopted a resolution in the same spirit and, in 1984, the Parti Québécois continues to propose turning Québec into an independent state based on the presidential model.

American and Québécois ideological similarities are another facet of Québec's nationalistic theory. In the annexation crisis of 1849, some Quebecers saw a chance to join the United States. In 1867, adversaries of Confederation advocated unity with the United States, and during the 1970's, the concept of a Québécois-American common market policy was very attractive to many.

If certain "Canadians" proclaimed, from American territory, the Republics of Upper and Lower Canada, some Americans proclaimed, on Canadian soil, the Republic of Indian Stream. After the Treaty of Paris in 1783, the border area between Canada and New Hampshire, although clearly defined, was for more than sixty years, coveted by both governments. In the absence of an officially recognized jurisdiction, the territory became a haven for cattle rustlers. In order to insure themselves of better protection, the colonists of the area proclaimed the Republic of Indian Stream in 1832. The citizenry rapidly became divided, and New Hampshire took advantage of the situation to interfere in the affairs of the young republic. The Webster-Ashburton Treaty gave the American government jurisdiction over these townships which, historically, had been Canadian territory.

The United States — The New Economic Metropolis

The first economic links between Canada and the United States took place around the middle of the last century. Canada, unhappy with the advent of the free-trade system recommended by England, sought a solution to its problems in economic reciprocity with the United States. This reciprocity also had another goal. It was envisaged that western American grain exports would follow the Great Lakes — Saint-Laurent route. The naval construction sector and the forest industry of New Brunswick supported the measure. Only the Maritime fishermen, fearing the loss of their monopoly to the Americans, opposed reciprocity.

The outbreak of the Crimean War in 1854 obliged England to avoid any conflict in America. The economic crisis engendered by the dropping of protectionist policies, as well as mounting tension between American and Canadian fishermen, finally resulted in the signing of a reciprocity treaty between Canada and the United States in 1854.

This treaty had a planned duration of ten years. Customs duties on natural products such as wood and wheat were suspended. Canada obtained navigational rights to Lake Michigan. In return, Americans were authorized to fish in Canadian territorial waters and to navigate the Saint-Laurent.

In 1866, the United States refused to renew the agreement. They were unhappy over England's attitude during the Civil War, the fact that manufactured goods were excluded from the treaty, the competition with the American transporters, and indirect increases in customs duties.

The Canadians saw in the American refusal one more reason to confederate. On July 1st, 1867, Canada was created.

The failure of reciprocity with the United States did not, however, signify the end of commercial and diplomatic relations between the two countries. In 1871, the Treaty of Washington eased the particularly strained climate between England and the United States at the time of the Civil War and, by eliminating all threat of war, facilitated the integration of the North American economy.

The continentalization of the North American economy had started with the creation of the free exchange system. The gradual withdrawal of England in the 1840's had led Canadians to look for new economic avenues. They opted for a continental system. New commercial centres in New York, Montréal, and the Great Lakes region replaced the old centres oriented toward the Atlantic. The canalization of the Saint-Laurent and the effects of the new economic structure accentuated the shift of the economy toward the centre of the country, to the detriment of cities to the east, including Québec. A vast railroad network, developed for a continental economy, completed the earlier existing river infrastructures. Before the end of the century, the United States had, in fact, replaced Great Britain as Canada's major economic partner.

Between 1850 and 1920, some 500 000 Québécois emigrated to the United States. Too numerous for small pieces of land, the Québécois went south to try to earn a better living. Attracted by the factories, they took the traditional invasion routes, but in the opposite direction. Many settled in the New England States. They found jobs in cotton spinning mills, in brick-making factories, and in the shoemaking industry. They created "little Canadas" on American soil. Their arrival in the United States coincided with the frenchifying of the Eastern Townships, and they dreamed of a new Francophone America which would stretch from Boston up to Québec City.

The Franco-Americans are still present in the New England States. They make up one-third of the population of Maine, Vermont, and New Hampshire. More than 3,1 million citizens of New England and New York State are of French descent. The French community of the American northeast is the largest in the United States. Louisiana, where the Acadians settled after being driven out of their birthplace (Nova Scotia) by the English at the time of the Conquest, has a million inhabitants of French origin, while California and Michigan have 1,3 million and 943 000, respectively. There are a half a million in each of Texas, Florida, Illinois, and Ohio. In the 1980 census, 13,6 million Americans indicated that they were of French, French-Canadian, or Acadian origin.[5] In 1983, the fourth biggest Canadian city, after Toronto, Montréal, and Vancouver was... Los Angeles with 850 000 inhabitants of Canadian origin (about 10 percent of the population) of whom 80 000 are Francophone. There are provincial associations, a Canada-California Chamber of Commerce, and a Quebec-California association. Most people are the descendants of explorers, soldiers, fur-traders, and gold-seekers who had once travelled over America on behalf of France and the Catholic Church. Up until 1760, Québec had been the capital of this French America and the Bishop of Québec had authority over the whole of North America.

The establishment of good economic relations between Canada and the United States continued into the 20th century. In 1911, the election again revolved around the question of economic reciprocity between the two countries. After World War I, Americans invested more in Canada than did the British. "From 1913 to 1926, the total capital invested in Canada coming from the United Kingdom went from 2 818 000$ to 2 637 000$. During the same period, the value of American investments in the country increased from 835 000$ to 3 196 000$."[6]

At the turn of the century, the United States had become a world power. American capitalism, which had saturated its own territory, had to find other new possibilities for investment. Canada, whose political and economic institutions resembled those of the United States, became an attractive market. Cultural and political affinities brought the two peoples together. England, interested in other markets and weakened by the First World War, let her North American colonies increasingly fend for themselves. The United States filled the void.

The United States and Canada's International Status

At the turn of the century, Canadian diplomacy was still under London's control. The Governor-General of Canada was advised that "the Dominion could not negotiate independantly with foreign powers while, at the same time, reaping the benefits of being part of the Empire."[7] Such an indirect influence was not always advantageous. It must be remembered that England had been very generous to the United States during the previous century, which had led to inconvenient delays.

"Let's say," declared half-seriously the American Secretary of State Elihu Root (1905-1909), "that I make a proposition to the British ambassador to the United States. He will have it sent to the Ministry of Foreign Affairs in London, who will then send it on to the Colonial Office who in turn will send it to the Government in Ottawa. (Root forgot to mention that the dispatch would be addressed to the Governor-General who would send it to the Privy Council who, in turn, would decide which minister would take care of it; finally, Sir Wilfrid Laurier would find the time to take care of it.)"[8]

The gradual withdrawal of British investments in Canada, and, to some extent, the fact that the United States replaced England as Canada's chief economic partner, would allow Canadians to acquire a greater independence in foreign politics.

In 1878, the Canadian government had, for the first time, expressed its reticence in financing the wars of the British Empire. Four years later, at the time of the Anglo-Egyptian conflict, Canadian "travellers" were recruited for transport ships on the Nile. But the men were hired with civilian contracts, and the Canadian government did not defray the cost. The small imperial wars were no longer Canada's business. At the time of the Boer War (1899-1902), the Canadian government allowed volunteers to be sent, not without having affirmed the right of Canada to decide if it would or would not take part in Great Britain's wars. In 1907, Laurier's government negociated a commercial treaty with the French government. The British ambassador did not take part in the negotiations. This was also the case with regard to a treaty signed with Japan a few years later. The Canadian delegate went to Tokyo without credentials officially issued by London. In 1909, the Canadian government created a Ministry of External Affairs. Several years later, the government refused to grant ships to England. Canada's participation in World War I accelerated the bringing about of Canadian independence. If the colonies had to take part in the war, they also had the right to participate in the drawing up of peace treaties. At the war's end, the Prime Ministers of the Dominions signed the Treaty of Versailles on behalf of their respective governments.

At the start of the 1920's, the question of renewing the Anglo-Japanese Alliance allowed the Canadian government to take a stand which was definitely different from England's diplomatic position. England wished to renew the agreement. Canada, knowing that the Americans were opposed to it, refused. The question was taken up again. The alliance was replaced by new, "very diplomatic" considerations, to the great satisfaction of the United States.

In 1922, at the time of the "Chanak" Incident, the Canadian government replied in a very evasive manner to an urgent call for help from the British government which was on the verge of declaring war on Turkey. A year later, a treaty between the United States and Canada dealing with halibut fishing was signed without its being initialed by the British ambassador. It was an important precedent.

Canada was becoming more and more an independent nation: Senator Dandurand became the President of the League of Nations Assembly in 1925, and Canada was elected to its council in 1927. The same year, a plenipotentiary minister was appointed in Washington. For the first time, a Canadian ambassador presented his credentials from Ottawa to a foreign government, that of the United States. In 1928, a plenipotentiary minister was appointed to Paris and the following year another was appointed to Tokyo. The United States, France, and Japan sent delegations to Ottawa. In 1931, the Statute of Westminster finally recognized the total independence of Canada.

Prestigious Visitors

On July 26, 1923, a crowd estimated at over 250 000 people greeted the American President Warren Harding in Vancouver. With the exception of President Chester Arthur (1881-1885) who, much to Washington's embarrassement, had accidentally ventured into Canadian waters during a fishing expedition in 1882, Harding was the first president ever to visit Canada. This was an important gesture and a sign of a new era in Canadian-American relations. Of the Canadian Prime Ministers, John A. MacDonald, in 1871, was the first to go to the United States.

The establishment of good relations between Canada and the United States brought new visitors. Tourists followed the soldiers. At the end of the last century, wealthy Americans began another "invasion", this time as tourists from Niagara Falls to chûte Montmorency. In Québec City, they admired the fortifications of the only fortified city in North America, and they marvelled at the city's European and French atmosphere. They also found a site where a important part of their own history had taken place.

It was at that time that the region of Charlevoix was starting to become a popular place to spend one's holidays. The famous Chisholm's Guide invited tourists to discover the area. Different boat excursions leaving from Toronto or New York were mentioned in it. Some say the Murray Bay Golf Course, opened in 1876, is the oldest in North America. It gave a certain prestige to the region.

William Howard Taft spent his summers there before becoming President of the United States in 1908. His memories of the area were unforgettable. There is no place like Murray Bay.... "If I only have one term, as seems likely in view of the complications that will be presented during that term, one of the great consolations will be that I can go to Murray Bay in the summers thereafter."

The admiration was mutual. The people of Charlevoix loved Taft. September 15, Taft's birthday, coincided with the end of the summer season. After the celebrations, everyone made plans to meet again the following year.

Starting in the 1920's, thanks to the invention of the automobile and the possibility of holidays for all, tourism became more and more important. In 1928, some 500 000 people, mostly American, are said to have visited Québec City. A Québec-American friendship was born. Upon the occasion of the three hundredth anniversary of the founding of Québec City in 1908 and the 1934 festivities commemorating the discovery of Canada, the Americans were invited to the ceremonies. After having fought for more than three centuries, Americans, French, Canadians, and Quebecois were finally reconciled.

World War II

The political context at the time of the Second World War and during the Cold War brought Canadians and Americans closer together. A solid friendship bound Mackenzie King, the Prime Minister of Canada, and Franklin D. Roosevelt, the President of the United States. Roosevelt knew Canada well. His family owned a summer home in Campobello, New Brunswick, and, as a young child, he spent his vacations there. It was during a boating trip that he fell into the icy waters of the Bay of Fundy and contracted poliomyelitis, from which he would suffer for the rest of his life.

On August 18, 1938, President Roosevelt, upon receiving an honourary diploma from Queen's University, declared that "the Dominion of Canada is part of the family which makes up the British Empire. I give to you the assurance that the people of the United States will not stand idly by if domination of Canadian soil is threatened by any other empire."[10] After the economy, the defence of North America became a continental affair.

On September 3, 1938, England declared war on Germany. Canada followed suit, but on September 10. On the 5th, Roosevelt, in an official declaration, excluded Canada from the belligerent countries. The gesture represented official recognition of Canadian autonomy with respect to England. It also permitted the British, it seems, to send war orders via Canada to the United States, which, given the laws governing trade, could not do business with a belligerent country.

During the war, economic, political, and military agreements became more and more frequent between the two countries. In August 1940, following the meeting at Ogdensburg, Canada and the United States decided jointly to insure North American defence. Prime Minister King was the only head of state besides the British Prime Minister to be aware of the American nuclear plan. The Japanese attack on Pearl Harbour made the United States aware of its vulnerability. Canada was increasingly becoming an area of strategic importance. The Americans built many defense installations here, most of which were not under the Canadian government's control. It is said that at the end of the war, the Americans wanted to charge the Canadians for their work. The figure was so high that the government, stupefied, asked them to lower it considerably so as not to annoy the Canadian people.

The agreements continued after the war. In 1949, Canada ratified the NATO pact, established for the defence of the North Atlantic and, on May 12, 1958, she accepted the NORAD agreements which put the American and Canadian air forces under the same command.

In Recent years...

After World War II, Canadian-American relations seemed to be at their best. There was more and more American investment in Canada. Canada had almost become the fifty-first American state. The rise of Canadian nationalism would quickly change things. The arrival of many immigrants of different cultures, the lower percentage of people of Anglo-Saxon origin in Canada, the need for Canadians to define themselves with respect to Québécois nationalism, and the wishes of a certain national bourgeoisie led Canadians to become more aware of themselves as a group.

At the height of the Cuban crisis, President Kennedy, faced with the danger of a war, declared a state of alert. The Prime Minister of Canada, John Diefenbaker, ill-informed of the goings-on behind the Russian-American crisis and in a spirit of independence, hesitated to alert the Canadian armed forces, as was demanded by the NORAD agreement. The act was perceived by Kennedy as being openly anti-American. The two politicians hardly ever agreed. Diefenbaker had been elected in 1957 on a strongly nationalistic platform. Disagreements about Canada's trading with Cuba had already taken place, and they continued after the Castro Revolution. It is said that, once, when Diefenbaker was visiting the White House, Kennedy had a painting put up that clearly intimated that the American army had been victorious over the Anglo-Canadian army during the War of 1812. In the early 1960's, the Canadian government led by Diefenbaker recalled its ambassador from Washington to protest against a note written by the American government which criticized the Canadian attitude on continental defence. This action embittered once again Canadian-American relations.

In April 1963, the election of Lester Pearson as Canadian Prime Minister healed old wounds. His relations with Kennedy were very cordial. But American foreign policy, different positions on the war in Vietnam, the growth of Canadian nationalism, the arrival of new economic partners, the questioning of American leadership throughout the world, border disputes, and the acid rain question would once again cloud relations between the two countries.

Beyond official politics, Americans, Canadians, and Québécois are still important partners. Canada and Québec have established several delegations in the United States. Exchanges are as numerous as ever. In 1980, more than 506 871 American tourists visited Québéc City. During the first four months of 1983, close to 1,2 million Canadians went to the United States. The attraction of the American lifestyle, as conveyed in films, television, literature, and sports, is ever-present. In a survey done in 1982, to the question, "If one day you were forced to emigrate outside of Québec and if you could choose only one of the following three places (Europe, Canada, the United States) which would you choose", 17,6% of those surveyed chose Europe, 45,6% elsewhere in Canada, and 26,7% the United States.[11]

John F. Kennedy, describing Canadian-American relations said, once, "Geography has made us neighbours. History has made us friends. Economics has made us partners. And necessity has made us allies."

Conclusion

... and the traveller returned along Chemin du Roy with his mind full of fond memories. He would have liked to taste just once more *Anguilles fumées, Saumoneaux dentelles, Poulet en gelée à la mode de l'Intendant, Gâteau mousseline érablière....* He would have liked to spend a few more wistful moments on the Remparts, "to walk down rue Saint-Jean once again", or to stroll through this city where Old France still lives.... "I'll be back." Québec will be waiting.

References

INTRODUCTION

1. Roy, Pierre-Georges, *La ville de Québec sous le Régime français*, Vol. 1, Québec, 1930, p.V.
2. Chouinard, François-Xavier, *La ville de Québec. Histoire municipale, 1. Régime français*, Québec, La Société historique de Québec, 1963, p. 12.
3. Gard, Anson Albert, *The Yankee in Quebec*, 1901, p. 197-198.

QUÉBEC THROUGH THE CENTURIES

1. ___________ Rapport du comité des Armoiries de la Cité de Québec, Québec, 1949, p. 1.
2. Trudel, Marcel, *Histoire de la Nouvelle-France. Les vaines tentatives 1534-1603*, Montréal, Fides, 1963, p. 103.
3. *Ibid.*, p. 104.
4. *Ibid.*, p. 105-106.
5. *Ibid.*, p. 259.
6. *Ibid.*, p. 262.
7. Larouche, Georges-Gauthier et Jean Claude Hébert, *L'habitation de Québec 1608-1615. Origine de l'établissement français en Amérique du Nord*, Beauport, 1982, p. 17.
8. *Ibid.*, p. 21
9. Paré, Jean, « Le vrai maire de Montréal voudrait-il se lever? » *Actualité*, Montréal, novembre 1982, p. 9.
10. Brown, Clément, *Québec, croissance d'une ville*, Québec, 1949, p. 50.
11. ___________ *Une ville à vendre*, Québec, Les Presses de l'Université Laval, 1981, p. 98.
12. Blanchard, Raoul, *L'est du Canada-français*, Tome II, Montréal, Beauchemin, 1935, p. 242.
13. ___________ *Nos Racines. Histoire vivante des Québecois*, Montréal, Les Éditions T.L.M. Inc., No 80, 1979, p. 1585-1586.
14. Comeau, Robert et al., *Économie québécoise*, Montréal, Les Presses de l'Université du Québec, 1969, p. 227.
15. Robert, Lionel, *Le port de Québec et l'économie de la zone métropolitaine de Québec*, 1978, p. 40.
16. Blanchard, Raoul, *L'est du Canada-français, Tome II*, Montréal, Beauchemin 1935, p. 40.
17. Direction générale du tourisme. Ministère de l'industrie, du commerce et du tourisme, *L'industrie touristique dans la région administrative de Québec (03)*, Québec, 1983, p. 4.
18. Delalande, Vianney, *Québec métropolitain*, Québec, Université Laval, 1968, p. 197.
19. Communauté urbaine de Québec, *Metro Quebec Canada Data*, 1980, p. 15.
20. *Ibid.*, p. 26.
21. Routhier, A.B., *Québec et Lévis à l'aurore du XXe siècle*, Montréal, 1900, p. 2.

FOOTLOOSE IN QUÉBEC: FIRST PART

1. Larouche, Georges-Gauthier et Jean-Claude Hébert, *L'habitation de Québec 1608-1615. Origine de l'établissement français en Amérique du Nord*, Beauport, 1982, p. 17.
2. Trudel, Marcel, « Champlain », *Dictionnaire biographique du Canada* Vol. 1 De l'an 1000 à 1700, Québec, P.U.L. 1967, p. 198.

3. Bertrand, Réal, *L'École Normale Laval* (1857-1957), Cahier d'histoire No. 9, La Société historique de Québec, 1957, p. 7.
4. Chouinard, François-Xavier, *La ville de Québec. Histoire municipale. 1. Régime français*, Québec, La Société historique de Québec, 1963, p. 103.
5. Duval, Monique, « L'intérêt pour la Place d'Armes n'est pas nouveau », *Le Soleil*, 16 août 1972, p. 47.
6. Bonenfant, Jean-Charles, « 1864: la Conférence de Québec fut aussi une fête mondaine », *Le Magazine Maclean*, novembre 1964, p. 46-47.
7. Pouliot, J. Camille, *Historical Reminder, Quebec and the Isle of Orleans* Québec, 1927, p. 170-171.
8. Kalm, Pehr, *Voyage de Pehr Kalm au Canada. 1749*, Traduction annotée du journal de route par Jacques Rousseau et al., Le Cercle du Livre de France 1977, p. 323.
9. Trudel, Marcel, *Initiation à la Nouvelle-France*, Montréal, 1971, p. 211.
10. Ouellet, Fernand, « Papineau et la rivalité Québec-Montréal (1820-1840) », *Revue d'histoire de l'Amérique française*, Vol. XIII, No 3, 1959, p. 313.
11. Paquet, Gilles et Jean-Pierre Wallot, « Le Bas-Canada au début du XIXe siècle: une hypothèse », *Revue d'histoire de l'Amérique française*, Vol., XXV, No 1, 1971, p. 40.
12. Brown, Clément, *Québec, croissance d'une ville*, Québec, 1949, p. 34.
13. *Ibid.*, p. 40.
14. Ministère des Affaires culturelles, Gouvernement du Québec, *La Place Royale deux siècles et demi d'histoire*, Québec, 1981, p. 15.
15. Hardy, René, *Aperçu du rôle religieux du curé de Notre-Dame de Québec (1840-1860)*, Thèse, Université Laval, 1968, p. 60.
16. Myrand, Ernest, *1690 Sir William Phips devant Québec. Histoire d'un siège*, Montréal, Beauchemin, 1925, p. 47.
17. Myrand, Ernest, *M. de la Colombière, Orateur. Historique d'un sermon célèbre...* Montréal, 1898, p. 31-32.
18. Lemay, Hugolin, *Vieux papiers, Vieilles chansons*, Montréal, 1936, p. 55.
19. Leclerc, Eugène, *Statistiques rouges*, Québec, 1932, p. 46.
20. *Idem.*
21. Noppen, Luc et al., Québec. *Trois siècles d'architecture*, Éditions Libre Expression, 1979, p. 37.
22. Roy, Pierre-Georges, *La ville de Québec sous le Régime français*. Vol. 1, Québec, 1930, p. 269.
23. ——————— *Voyage au Canada dans le nord de l'Amérique septentrionale fait depuis l'an 1751 à 1761* par J.C.B., Québec, 1887, p. 21.
24. Hamelin, Jean et Jean Provencher, « La vie de relation sur le Saint-Laurent entre Québec et Montréal au milieu du XVIIIe siècle », *Cahier de Géographie de Québec*, Vol. XXIII, 1967, p. 246.
25. Roby, Yves et Jean Hamelin, *Histoire économique du Québec*, 1851-1896. Montréal, Fides, 1971, p. 126.
26. Sewell, Édouard William, *Rapport sur un pont suspendu projeté pour le passage d'un chemin de fer et pour la traverse du fleuve fait à son honneur le Maire et au Conseil de Ville de Québec*, Québec, 1853, p. 60.
27. Boucher, Georges-A., *Je me souviens*, Montréal, Arbour et Dupont, 1933, p. 94-95.
28. Roy, Pierre-Georges, *La traversée entre Québec et Lévis*, Lévis, 1942, p. 4.
29. *Ibid.*, p. 41.
30. ——————— *The Plains of Abraham*, 1899, p. 1.
31. Beaudet, Louis, *Québec ses monuments anciens et modernes...* Cahier d'histoire no 25, La Société historique de Québec, 1973, p. 45.

FOOTLOOSE IN QUÉBEC: SECOND PART

1. Pouliot, Léon, « Lalement, Gabriel », *Dictionnaire Biographique du Canada.* Vol. 1, De l'an 1000 à 1700. Les Presses de l'Université Laval, 1966, p. 425.
2. Linteau, Paul-André et al., *Histoire du Québec contemporain. De la Confédération à la crise. (1867-1929)* Boréal-Express, 1979, p. 235.
3. Noppen, Luc et al., Québec. *Trois siècles d'architecture.* Éditions Libre Expression, 1979, p. 392.
4. Bouchette, Joseph, *Description Topographique de la province du Bas-Canada avec des remarques sur le Haut-Canada...*, Londres, 1815, p. 466.
5. Vaugeois, Denis et al., *Canada-Québec. Synthèse historique*, Ottawa, Éditions du Renouveau Pédagogique Inc., 1973, p. 194.
6. Savard, Pierre, *La ville de Québec au miroir de la littérature (1860-1900)*, Québec, La Société historique de Québec, 1971, p. 14.
7. ——————— *Montréal-Fin-De-Siècle*, Montréal, 1899, p. 53.
8. Trudel, Marcel, « Cartier, Jacques », *Dictionnaire Biographique du Canada*, Vol. 1, De l'An 1000 à 1700, Les Presses de l'Université Laval, 1966, p. 173.
9. Kalm, Pehr, *Voyage de Pehr Kalm au Canada en 1749.* Traduction annotée du Journal de route par Jacques Rousseau et al., Montréal, 1977, p. 315.
10. Pépin, Jacques, « L'inhumation de la dépouille du Carnaval de Montréal », *L'Événement Journal*, Québec, 7 mars 1962, p. 16.
11. Duval, Monique, « L'histoire de l'anesthésie à Québec a débuté en 1848, » *Le Soleil*, mercredi 25 novembre 1970, p. 11.
12. ——————— *Nos Racines. L'histoire vivante des Québécois*, Montréal, Les Éditions T.L.M. Inc., No 26, 1979, p. 496.
13. Rivet, Monique, *Les Irlandais à Québec 1870-1968*, Thèse, Université Laval, 1969, p. 7.
14. Massicotte, E.Z. *Faits curieux de l'histoire de Montréal*, Montréal, Beauchemin, 1922, p. 66-67.

QUÉBEC CITY AND THE NORTH AMERICAN CONTINENT

1. Trudel, Marcel, « Enfin les fleurs de lis, 1524 », *Revue d'histoire de l'Amérique française*, Vol. XV, No 4. 1962, p. 490.
2. Lacour-Gayet, *Histoire des États-Unis. Des origines à la fin de la guerre civile*, Fayard, p. 107-108.
3. Martin, Lawrence, *The Presidents and the Prime Ministers*, Toronto, 1982, p. 32.
4. Lederman, W.R., « Notre héritage commun. Autre temps... autre constitution, » *Perspectives internationales*, 1976, p. 26.
5. ——————— « 13 millions de cousins aux États-Unis », *Le Soleil*, 7 décembre 1983, p. E-13.
6. Sales, Arnaud, *La bourgeoisie industrielle au Québec*, Québec, P.U.F., 1979, p. 165.
7. Soward, F.H., *Le ministère des affaires extérieures et l'autonomie canadienne 1899-1939*, La Société historique du Canada, Brochure historique, No 7, 1956, p. 3.
8. *Idem.*
9. Martin, Lawrence, *The Presidents and the Prime Ministers*, Toronto, 1982, p. 68.
10. *Ibid.*, p. 127.
11. Hogue, Jean-Pierre, *L'héritage de Jacques Cartier. Les valeurs, l'appartenance et les frustrations des Québécois*, Montréal, Inedi, 1982, p. 11.

Index

F

G

H

I

J

K

L

M

N

O

P

Q

R

S

T

V

W